The People's Quest for Leadership in Church and State

Praise for Frank Brennan's *Amplifying That Still Small Voice:*

Frank Brennan says he wants to be an ambassador for conscience. I say he is a shining light. Frank has never let the still, small voice of conscience be silenced either by self-interest or by unquestioning acceptance of authority.
   -Kristina Keneally, ex-Premier of NSW

Frank can say things that no bishop can say, and to audiences which would invite no bishop to speak. The public Church needs him. The need for his presence in the Australian public square is so obvious.
   -Bishop Greg O'Kelly SJ AM

Any time is the right time to have an intelligent voice raised in the community and in the Church. But now is a crucial time to hear Frank Brennan's discerning voice.
   -Fr Michael Elligate

Frank's experience of listening to the still, small voices of people on the margins, has given him great authenticity in amplifying those voices.
   -Brother Sean McManus cfc

Thanks to the work and advocacy of Frank Brennan as seen in his work in the public forum, justice has been kept as a 'constitutive' dimension of preaching the Gospel.
   -Bishop William Morris

The People's Quest
for
Leadership
in Church and State

Frank Brennan SJ

ATF Theology
Adelaide
2015

Text copyright © 2015 remains with Frank Brennan SJ.

All rights reserved. Except for any fair dealing permitted under the Copyright Act, no part of this book may be reproduced by any means without prior permission. Inquiries should be made to the publisher.

National Library of Australia Cataloguing-in-Publication

creator: Brennan, Frank, 1954- author.

Title: The people's quest for leadership in church and state /

Frank Brennan.

ISBN: 9781925232578 (paperback)
        9781925232585 (hardback)
        9781925232592 (ebook : kindle)
        9781925232608 (ebook : pdf)

Notes: Includes index.

Subjects: Christian leadership--Catholic Church.

Political leadership--Australia

Church and state--Australia--Catholic Church.

Dewey Number: 262.1

Cover design and Layout/Artwork by Astrid Sengkey
Photo of Frank Brennan by Julia Charles
Text Minion Pro Size 10 &11

Published by:

An imprint of the ATF Ltd.
PO Box 504
Hindmarsh, SA 5007
ABN 90 116 359 963
www.atfpress.com
Making a lasting difference

Dedicated
to
Sir William Deane

Judge, Governor-General, leader, mentor, and friend

'There is one challenge for the future leaders of our nation which I would particularly emphasise. It is the challenge of justice and truth. The challenge never to be indifferent in the face of injustice or falsehood. It encompasses the challenge to advance truth and human dignity rather than to seek advantage by inflaming ugly prejudice and intolerance.'

-Sir William Deane

on the occasion of the awarding of an honorary degree
by the University of Queensland, 29 May 2003

Table of Contents

Foreword
Paul Bongiorno AM   xi

Introduction   xv

Leadership in the Church

1. Educating for Justice   3
2. Discerning the Appropriate Path   13
3. Getting the Structures and Processes Right   17
4. Being inspired by Our Modern Martyrs   29
5. Looking to Our Local Prophets   33

Leadership of the Nation

6. The Light on the Hill   41
7. The Spirit of ANZAC   65
8. The Enigma of Malcolm Fraser   71
9. The Quirkiness of Wayne Goss   75
10. The Grandeur of Gough Whitlam   77

Conclusion   81

Index   85

Foreword

In his Pulitzer prize winning history, *Profiles In Courage*, a young United States Senator John F Kennedy wrote, 'In a democracy, every citizen, regardless of his interest in politics, "holds office"; every one of us is in a position of responsibility; and in the final analysis, the kind of government we get depends upon how we fulfil those responsibilities. We, the people are the boss, and we will get the kind of political leadership, be it good or bad, that we demand and deserve.'

Those sentiments are a chilling judgment on the malaise many Australians believe they are enduring thanks to an appalling descent into the banal and the short term that passes for leadership in this country. Slogans that appeal to the basest of prejudices and selfishness betray the very founding values we as citizens most prize: a democratic pluralist society where the rule of law protects individual freedoms, where compassion is the measure of the polity and tolerance its hallmark.

Kennedy's study of six American politicians documents the enormous price they paid for having the courage to do what they were convinced was right. Loss of office, loss of friendship, loss of esteem. Some were rewarded with reinstatement years later. Their causes, like the abolition of slavery, vindicated.

It is not that Australia has not got its own profiles in courage. A Chifley, Whitlam, Fraser, a Goss are cited in these reflections.

Journalist Van Badham writing for *The Guardian* observes, 'Political leadership operates at the intersection of policy imagination, strength and resilience, team management, insight into the political moment and the ability to communicate with appreciable sincerity.

Whitlam, Hawke, Keating and Howard possessed these talents. Rudd to his shame and Gillard to her tragedy, did not.'

Where was the courage of Kevin Rudd to go to a double dissolution election over the rejection of the prescription he told the nation was needed to address climate change? It was after all, 'the biggest moral challenge of our lifetime.' Based on the template of Gough Whitlam back in 1974 I believed Rudd had no option and said so on radio and television. I was gobsmacked when he baulked. There would be no universal health insurance, no Medicare, if Whitlam had shown the same cynical timidity. Not that the cynicism was all one sided. The playing off of the planet's future against short term rises in electricity bills was breathtaking in its myopia.

For Catholics of course there is an intersection between leadership of Church and state. The project that Ben Chifley laid out for the Labor Party in his famous Light On The Hill speech gives expression to the Gospel based option for the poor. The qualities of leadership demanded of our politicians are also demanded of our church leaders. Indeed both are striving to ensure the health, well-being and happiness of the same society.

Traditionally it has been argued that the Catholic Church is not a democracy. Even if we concede this, just as firmly it is not an absolute monarchy. It is, as Vatican II and Pope Francis insist a community of believers. Each baptised person conscientiously brings his or her insights and gifts to its mission and understanding of itself. It is surely time for these voices—male and female—to be heard. This conciliar view of the church with firm historic roots is at stark odds with current Canon Law. At Canon 1404 we have enshrined an unaccountable authority: 'The First See (the Bishop of Rome) is judged by no one.'

This authoritarian top down model has served contemporary Australian Catholics very badly. There's been the appointment of men as bishops who see their leadership role in narrow clericalist terms. They are agents of what has been a secretive and anachronistic Roman curia. Never to question but simply to impose rigid prescriptions that exclude rather than include people. So the tenor and collegiality message of the current Pope is for many of them a culture shattering earthquake.

Pope Francis, like any effective leader, 'secular' or 'sacred' puts real people in real situations ahead of narrow ideology or theology. He seeks to read the 'signs of the times'. To discern the activity of the Spirit in good people who love and sacrifice and who are, at the same time, gay or divorced and remarried.

There is a real chance that as far as many Australian Catholics are concerned the Church has already forfeited credible leadership. They find little or no acknowledgement of their real life situations from the bishops. No public acknowledgement of contemporary reality like the German bishops in their response to Pope Francis: 'In most cases where the church's teaching is known, it is only selectively accepted. The idea of the sacramental marriage covenant, which encompasses faithfulness and exclusivity on the part of the spouses and the transmission of life, is normally accepted by people who marry in the church. Most of the baptised enter into marriage with the expectation and hope of concluding a bond for life. The church's statements on premarital sexual relations, on homosexuality, on those divorced and remarried, and on birth control, by contrast, are virtually never accepted, or are expressly rejected in the vast majority of cases.'

Leaders whether they be ecclesiastical or secular who are perceived to be out of touch or just incapable of 'getting it' are doomed to failure. If a political leader abandons the future and is seen to be selling out the nation for narrow sectional interest, the judgement at the ballot box will be harsh. When it comes to the church the only real option is for people to vote with their feet. And they are doing it.

There are prophets in our midst. Leaders who show courage and resonate. The sacked bishop of Toowoomba, Bill Morris, is one. The retired auxiliary bishop of Sydney, Geoffrey James Robinson, is another. And without a doubt, Prime Minister Keating's 'meddling priest' fits the bill. Frank Brennan has also been described by Kevin Rudd as 'an ethical burr in the nation's saddle'. Like the fourteenth century saint, Catherine of Sienna who chided the Avignon Pope, he is also an ethical burr in the saddle of the Australian church, and thank God for that.

Paul Bongiorno AM

Introduction

I was spending an academic year in Boston when former Australian Prime Ministers' Gough Whitlam and then Malcolm Fraser died. I avidly watched their funeral services on my computer. Gough's event at Sydney Town Hall was marked by a certain grandeur and the finest oratory espousing his public achievements. The nation had come of age with the Aboriginal leader Noel Pearson saluting 'this old man for his great love and dedication to his country and to the Australian people'.

Malcolm's service at the Scots' Church in Melbourne was marked by family tributes and the silent expression of thanks by the Vietnamese refugees on the steps of the Church. His daughter Phoebe Wynn-Pope applied to Fraser the remarks of Theodore Roosevelt when reflecting on great leadership:

> Credit belongs to the man who has actually been in the arena . . . whose face is marred by dust and sweat and blood; who strives valiantly; who errs, who comes short again and again, because there is no effort without error and shortcoming; but who does actually strive to do the deeds; who knows great enthusiasms, the great devotions; who spends himself in a worthy cause; who at the best knows in the end the triumph of high achievement.

We had lost two fine leaders—ex-prime ministers who led the country in its moral reflections on difficult issues such as the treatment of asylum seekers, and long after they had left elected office. When in the Australian Federal Parliament, they had become mortal enemies. After their lives in parliament, they maintained their robust differences over the events of the 1975 Dismissal while finding common ground on vexed moral and political issues. They spoke with moral authority but without talking down to their audiences. They challenged contemporary elected leaders but without taking to the bully pulpit where the impotent are pure. They maintained their comprehensive world views but without excluding from consideration or respect those who saw the world differently. In their going, I sensed that the nation had lost two elders who had become beacons for a people often lost amidst the partisan point-scoring of parliament's gladiatorial 'Question Time', the controlled diet of the tabloid media and the radio shock jocks, and the community's insular concern with economic self-interest and national security. Their appearances together on the national stage had helped call us beyond ourselves and look beyond the immediate horizon of the next Budget or election. The lost opportunities of the Rudd-Gillard years and the election of the Abbott government with the simplistic mantras of stopping the boats and axing the taxes provided a stark political background for their calls to nobler national action. In the darkness, they held out the promise of a light on the hill. I had cause to reflect on the light on the hill when delivering the 2103 Chifley oration in Bathurst.

Meanwhile the voice of the nation's religious leaders was muted or even silenced. The scandal of child sexual abuse in the churches was on daily display, including the failure of religious authorities to act promptly, transparently, compassionately and justly. Why would people listen to the moral counsel of the leaders of churches speaking about issues of national concern when they had failed to protect even children committed to their care, and when they seemed so slow to catch up with the community outrage at institutional cover-ups and oversights? However the new Pope Francis was striking chords even with the cynical and the estranged. Here was a pope very at home in his own skin, preaching a message of joy and hope, aligning himself unashamedly with the poor and marginalised. He knew the world had had enough of dogma and pedagogy and was crying out for pastoral solicitude. The spring in his step has been infectious. He has been able to provide a consoling reassurance that no matter what the enormity of the problems confronted, we human beings have the capacity to respond affirmatively and productively. He has held out Francis of Assisi as a model for all persons seeking 'the inseparable bond between concern for nature, justice for the poor, commitment to society, and interior peace'. No one in their right mind and with a right disposition would forego that bond or ridicule others who seek it. Taking on big intractable issues like climate change and the loss of biodiversity, Francis has declared, 'We lack leadership capable of striking out on new paths and meeting the needs of the present with concern for all and without prejudice towards coming generations.'[1]

While contemplating the deaths of Whitlam and Fraser in the wake of the 2013 federal election during the ANZAC Centenary, and welcoming the papacy of Francis in the wake of the child sexual abuse crisis, I have been reflecting on the quest for leadership in Church and State. I have returned to Australia convinced that we the people are seeking spiritual and political leaders who can inspire us to dedicate ourselves to taking up the burdens of the fallen and, with the same high courage and steadfastness with which they went into battle, to setting our hands to the tasks they left unfinished (some of which they could not possibly have imagined a century ago), and giving our utmost to make the world what they would have wished it to be —a better and happier place for all of its people, through whatever means are open to us. Those future leaders are in our midst. As well as being bloodied and tested, they need to be nurtured, encouraged, and espoused. That is the modest purpose of this slight collection of writings and addresses delivered from Bathurst to Boston and back to Melbourne and Sydney.

---

1. Pope Francis, *Laudato Si'*, #10, 53.

Leadership in the Church

1

Educating for Justice

This was an address to the Jesuit Higher Education International Network at Newman College, University of Melbourne in July 2015.

The land on which we meet here at Newman College was still an open paddock 100 years ago. It was the traditional land of the Wurundjeri people who had made their home here as hunters and gatherers for tens of thousands of years. The surrounding blocks were already the sites for the splendid university colleges erected by the other major Christian churches with a presence here at the University of Melbourne. You will understand that the Catholics, many of whom were Irish, did not yet have the means nor the vision for the building of their own college on the crescent adjacent to the university.

Sydney was founded well before Melbourne with the result that there was already a well established Catholic men's college at the University of Sydney. But not even Sydney had a college for Catholic women. Back in 1885, Cardinal Moran had cause to dismiss the then rector of Sydney's St John's College for 'levity of conduct with young ladies' as well as for low enrolments. I do not know how sustainable the rector's claim on his job would have been if enrolments had been healthier. When looking for a new college rector, Cardinal Moran could not afford to be too choosy. But he did rule out two classes of men: Englishmen and Jesuits. He regarded Jesuits as 'a law unto themselves'.[1]

---

1. Brenda Niall, *Mannix* (Melbourne : Text Publishing, 2015), 105.

When the legendary Irish cleric Daniel Mannix left Maynooth and came to Melbourne as coadjutor bishop to Archbishop Carr in 1913, Carr entrusted him with the mission of developing this vacant site. Brenda Niall, a splendid Australian biographer, has recently published a new life of Mannix. She was left in no doubt that Mannix had no interest in building a Catholic university, but rather saw the need for Catholics in the tertiary education sector to act as a leavening element in the thoughts and ideals of the developing secular universities. Unlike many other countries, Australia has long had a strong system of Catholic secondary schools but until recently no Catholic universities. I remember when the Provost of the newly established Australian Notre Dame University proudly told my father when he was Chief Justice of Australia that Notre Dame was about to establish Australia's first Catholic law school. Dad simply responded with a question, 'Must you?' We now have two Catholic universities in Australia. Much has changed since Mannix's day.

In a chapter entitled, 'Playing Poker with the Jesuits', Brenda Niall spells out Mannix's vision for Catholic tertiary education. He wanted to put Catholics (and that more than often meant Irish) 'on a footing similar to that of other denominations'. In 1910, Archbishop Carr had welcomed the Newman Society into his archdiocese so that it might have a presence here at the University of Melbourne. Brenda Niall opines that nothing much might have become of Mannix but for the 1916 Easter uprising at the post office in Dublin and the subsequent conscription campaigns in Australia where Mannix strongly and successfully opposed government moves for military conscription during the First World War.

Planning for Newman College, Mannix, unlike his Sydney episcopal brethren, wanted the Jesuits to do the job. It would have made sense for him to commission Fr James O'Dwyer SJ, then rector of Xavier College, the large Jesuit secondary school with place for boarders, to be the first rector. But alas, though Irish born, O'Dwyer was 'a King and Empire Man' who had told the Old Xavierians at the outbreak of the war that 'in the story of Empire there is nothing so unselfish as the relation of the Motherland to her colonies'.[2] This was too much for Mannix. Eventually he found another Jesuit for the task.

---

2. Niall, *Mannix*, 112.

Once assured a major donor from Sydney, Mannix took a very hands on approach to the construction of Newman College. He knew that architecture mattered. He made a bold choice, giving the job to an American couple, Walter Burley Griffin and his wife Marion Mahony. Brenda Niall observes that Mannix 'never liked being predictable and it would have pleased him to have the Catholic college, a latecomer to the University of Melbourne, make such a strong statement of individuality. Choosing between adventurous modernism and predictable neo-Gothic, Mannix would take the risk of the new, even at the cost of antagonising the major donor.'[3]

We are meeting in the splendid circular dining room. Thomas Donovan, the Sydney donor, disliked much about the building, but most especially the dining room. He thought it was designed to 'enforce equality'. That was the sort of thing Americans did! It was American, even socialist, in feeling. Niall interprets Donovan's displeasure: 'No humble approach to High Table, no dignity, nothing to signal the authority of the rector.'[4] Mannix was so delighted with the result that he became a great backer for Burley Griffin who then became the architect for Canberra, our national capital which is home for me and Newman's erstwhile rector Fr Peter L'Estrange. I often tell my American friends that Canberra is a bit like Washington DC, but without the power, money, influence and prestige.

On the far wall there is a regal portrait of Fr Jeremiah Murphy who was rector here for thirty years. He loved the place, and he was very at home engaging with the administration of the University of Melbourne. When his Provincial finally moved him to Xavier College, he wrote in his diary: 'Entered the desert'.[5] He died within a year, aged 71.

As a young Jesuit, I had a couple of brief stints at Newman College, tutoring in constitutional law. Kevin Andrews who is now the Australian Minister for Defence was president of the students' club. Kevin is part of a cabinet which contains a great number of alumni from Jesuit schools including the prime minister, the treasurer, the minister for finance, the minister for education and the minister for agriculture. And it almost goes without saying that the nation's chief

---

3. Niall, *Mannix*, 115.
4. Niall, *Mannix*, 116.
5. Niall, *Mannix*, 327.

justice and leader of the opposition also attended Jesuit schools. It is good for our corporate humility to acknowledge that the governor-general was educated by the Christian Brothers and that our Queen received no Catholic education at all, though she is of course not one of us, and she lives on the other side of the globe.

I suspect Pope Francis had some of our alumni in mind when he wrote in his encyclical *Laudato Si'*:

> A politics concerned with immediate results, supported by consumerist sectors of the population, is driven to produce short-term growth. In response to electoral interests, governments are reluctant to upset the public with measures which could affect the level of consumption or create risks for foreign investment. The myopia of power politics delays the inclusion of a far-sighted environmental agenda within the overall agenda of governments. Thus we forget that 'time is greater than space', that we are always more effective when we generate processes rather than holding on to positions of power. True statecraft is manifest when, in difficult times, we uphold high principles and think of the long-term common good. Political powers do not find it easy to assume this duty in the work of nation-building.[6]

Many of us were last gathered together five years ago in Mexico at this conference under the leadership and inspiration of the late Fr Paul Locatelli SJ to hear Fr General Adolfo Nicolas put three major challenges in response to what he called the pervasive 'globalisation of superficiality' by which we can be 'overwhelmed with such a dizzying pluralism of choices and values and beliefs and visions of life, then one can so easily slip into the lazy superficiality of relativism or mere tolerance of others and their views, rather than engaging in the hard work of forming communities of dialogue in the search of truth and understanding'. The Jesuit General said:

> First, in response to the globalisation of superficiality, I suggest that we need to study the emerging cultural world of our students more deeply and find creative ways of promoting depth of thought and imagination, a depth that is transformative of the person. Second, in order to maximise

---

6. Pope Francis, *Laudato Si'*, #178.

the potentials of new possibilities of communication and cooperation, I urge the Jesuit universities to work towards operational international networks that will address important issues touching faith, justice, and ecology that challenge us across countries and continents. Finally, to counter the inequality of knowledge distribution, I encourage a search for creative ways of sharing the fruits of research with the excluded; and in response to the global spread of secularism and fundamentalism, I invite Jesuit universities to a renewed commitment to the Jesuit tradition of learned ministry which mediates between faith and culture.[7]

Those of us inspired by the Jesuit tradition have once again gathered in the global South to consider the challenges put by the Jesuit Superior General. We mourn the loss of Paul Locatelli who died soon after our last conference reminding us: 'We must challenge the illusion of privilege and isolated individualism. We must bind ourselves emotionally and functionally to others and to the earth.'[8] This time we have gathered in Asia, though admittedly Australia is probably the least Asian country in South East Asia. Fr Peter C Phan the Georgetown theologian recently reflected on the Church in Asia which he describes as 'the cradle of the world's religions'. Profiling the concerns of the Federation of Asian Bishops Conference, Phan writes:

> The FABC's dominant concern is centred on the kingdom of God (not on the institutional church); mission (not inward-self-absorption); communion (not splendid isolation); dialogue (not imperialistic monologue); solidarity with victims (not victim-blaming and withdrawal into an otherworldly 'spirituality'); care of creation (not exploitation of natural resources); and witness/martyrdom (not cowardly compromise).[9]

---

7. Adolfo Nicolas, 'Depth, Universality, And Learned Ministry: Challenges To Jesuit Higher Education Today', Address to the 'Networking Jesuit Higher Education: Shaping the Future for a Humane, Just, Sustainable Globe' Conference, Mexico City, 22 April 2010 at
< http://www.scu.edu/scm/winter2010/shapingthefuture.cfm>.
8. Quoted by Fr Michael McCarthy SJ in his homily at the funeral of Paul Locatelli SJ on 16 July 2010, at <http://www.scu.edu/scm/winter2010/lastgoodbye.cfm>.
9. Peter C Phan, 'Reception of and Trajectories for Vatican II in Asia', in *50 Years On:*

We are now preparing for the 36th General Congregation of the Jesuits. And we are buoyed up by the leadership of our Jesuit Pope, Francis, who embodies so much of what we espouse and who challenges us to respond with full hearts, applied minds, and willing hands.

Remember how Pope Francis ended his address to the journalists in Rome on the day after his election when he gave a blessing with a difference. He said:

> I told you I was cordially imparting my blessing. Since many of you are not members of the Catholic Church, and others are not believers, I cordially give this blessing silently, to each of you, respecting the conscience of each, but in the knowledge that each of you is a child of God. May God bless you![10]

Now that is what I call a real blessing for anybody and everybody— and not a word of Vaticanese. Respect for the conscience of every person, regardless of their religious beliefs; silence in the face of difference; affirmation of the dignity and blessedness of every person; offering, not coercing; suggesting, not dictating; leaving room for gracious acceptance. These are all good pointers for members of the Jesuit Higher Education Network holding the treasure of the Ignatian tradition, Roman authority and Catholic ritual in trust for all people of good will, including all our staff and students, as we discern how best to make a home for God in our lives and in our world, assured that the Spirit of God has made her home with us.

Something crystallised for me at the splendid Sydney Opera House soon after the election of Francis when I appeared on stage with the British philosopher AC Grayling, author of *The God Argument*, and Sean Faircloth, the United States director of one of the Dawkins Institutes passionately committed to atheism. We were there to discuss their certainty about the absurdity of religious faith. Mr Faircloth raised what had already become a hoary old chestnut, the failure of Pope Francis when provincial of the Jesuits in Argentina during the Dirty Wars to adequately defend his fellow Jesuits who

---

Probing the Riches of Vatican II, edited by David G Schultenover (Collegeville: Liturgical Press, 2015), 312.
10. Pope Francis, Address to Members of Communications Media, 16 March 2013, <http://w2.vatican.va/content/francesco/en/speeches/2013/march/documents/papa-francesco_20130316_rappresentanti-media.html>.

were detained and tortured by unscrupulous soldiers. Being a Jesuit, I thought I was peculiarly well situated to respond. I confess to having got a little carried away. I exclaimed: 'Yes, how much better it would have been if there had been just one secular, humanist, atheist philosopher who had stood up in the city square in Buenos Aires and shouted, "Stop it!" The military junta would have collectively come to their senses, stopped it, and Argentinians would have lived happily ever after.' The luxury for such philosophers is that they never have to get their hands dirty and they think that religious people who do are hypocrites unless of course they take the course of martyrdom. As believers, we are able to hold together ideals and reality, commitment and forgiveness.

The voice of conscience missions the believer not just for service in the Church but most especially for service in the world, not just with commitment to justice in the Church but most especially to justice in the world. This cannot be done without a commitment to laws and policies which do justice, protecting the weak and vulnerable. It is a call to take an intelligent, informed stand in solidarity. In his encyclical Pope Francis calls us to consider the tragic effects of environmental degradation especially on the lives of the world's poorest. He says:

> The problem is that we still lack the culture needed to confront this crisis. We lack leadership capable of striking out on new paths and meeting the needs of the present with concern for all and without prejudice towards coming generations. The establishment of a legal framework which can set clear boundaries and ensure the protection of ecosystems has become indispensable, otherwise the new power structures based on the techno-economic paradigm may overwhelm not only our politics but also freedom and justice.[11]

Developing the culture, the leadership, and the legal framework. These are the challenges to those who want to be intelligent believers responding to the call of the Spirit. It is heartening to note Pope Francis's humility born of true consultation with bishops' conferences (seventeen of which are quoted directly in the encyclical) and detailed meetings with experts including scientists, economists and political scientists as well as philosophers and theologians. Having

---

11. Pope Francis, *Laudato Si'*, #53.

noted, 'There are certain environmental issues where it is not easy to achieve a broad consensus', he concedes that 'the Church does not presume to settle scientific questions or to replace politics. But I want to encourage an honest and open debate, so that particular interests or ideologies will not prejudice the common good'.[12]

Returning home to our universities and places of higher learning, we must commit all our institutions to engagement in this honest and open debate, respecting the competencies of all, and inspired by Pope Francis's vision of St Francis of Assisi who is the model of the inseparable bond 'between concern for nature, justice for the poor, commitment to society, and interior peace'.[13] Mind you, I do think the encyclical would be all the stronger if it conceded that the growth in the world's human population—from 2 billion when Pius XII first spoke of contraception to 3.5 billion when Paul VI promulgated *Humanae Vitae* to 7.3 billion and climbing as it is today—points to a need to reconsider the Church's teaching on contraception. The pope is quite right to insist that the reduction of population growth is not the only solution to the environmental crisis. But it is part of the solution. It may even be an essential part of the solution. Banning contraception in a world of 7.3 billion people confronting the challenges of climate change and loss of biodiversity is a very different proposition from banning it in a world of only 2 billion people oblivious of such challenges. I doubt that you would find any papal adviser today who would advocate that the planet's situation with climate change, loss of biodiversity, and water shortages would be improved if only all people of good will had declined to use artificial birth control for the last fifty years.

Celebrating the 50th anniversary of Vatican II and preparing for the forthcoming Synod on the Family, we can take heart from the changes in our Church which permit and encourage such questions and dialogue. One effect of the recent encyclical is that it is no longer just liberal Catholics who are labeled as cafeteria Catholics. Some erstwhile conservative Catholics and papal apologists have become very exceptionalist in their discussion of this encyclical. All are now welcome to the real world of questioning engagement in a Church that we cherish for its teaching office and sense of tradition. John O'Malley SJ, the finest contemporary historian of Vatican II writing

---

12. Pope Francis, *Laudato Si'*, #188.
13. Pope Francis, *Laudato Si'*, #11.

in the English language has provided us with 'a simple litany' of the changes in church style indicated by the council's vocabulary:

> from commands to invitations, from laws to ideals, from threats to persuasion, from coercion to conscience, from monologue to conversation, from ruling to serving, from withdrawn to integrated, from vertical and top-down to horizontal, from exclusion to inclusion, from hostility to friendship, from static to changing, from passive acceptance to active engagement, from prescriptive to principled, from defiant to open-ended, from behaviour modification to conversion of heart, from the dictates of law to the dictates of conscience, from external conformity to the joyful pursuit of holiness.[14]

As members of the Jesuit Higher Education Network committed to social justice we have great potential and vast material, intellectual and spiritual resources. But this is no time for self-satisfaction nor complacency. If you are in any doubt about that, consider only the London *Tablet* of 11 July 2015 which carries the front page headline: 'Are the Jesuits pulling out of Britain?'.[15] The closure of Heythrop College brings to an end a history that began in Louvain in Belgium in 1614, when it was illegal to educate Catholic priests in England. The original college in Louvain was made possible by the gift of a wealthy English benefactor. Four centuries later, its successor institution has now run out of benefactors. No institution is sacred. No institution is spared the scrutiny of accountants and bean counters.

Looking to the future, let's sustain each other in hope. Looking to the future, I conclude appropriately quoting one of our fine contemporary women theologians. In her new book *Ask the Beasts: Darwin and the God of Love*, Elizabeth A Johnson, writes: 'Living the ecological vocation in the power of the Spirit sets us off on a great adventure of mind and heart, expanding the repertoire of our love.'[16] We leave Newman College in Melbourne, Australia, grateful for the

---

14. John W O'Malley, 'Vatican II: Did Anything Happen?', in *Vatican II: Did Anything Happen?*, edited by David G Scholthoven,(London: Continuum, 2007), 81.
15. *The Tablet*, 11 July 2015.
16. Elizabeth A Johnson, *Ask the Beasts: Darwin and the God of Love* (London: Bloomsbury, 2014), 286.

vision of Mannix, inspired by the architecture of the Griffins, buoyed by the encyclical of our Jesuit Pope, and grounded in the realities that all this needs to be translated into the daily fare of fee paying education for students seeking employment in a globalised world back home.

2

Discerning the Appropriate Path

This was my 2015 homily for the feast of St Ignatius Loyola, the founder of the Jesuits. The readings for the day were Deuteronomy 30:15–20, 1 Corinthians 10:31–11:1, and Luke 14:25–33.

Once he had been hit by a cannon ball and was laid up in bed, Ignatius became rather expert in the choice offered by Moses to the people. Whether in the big things or little things of life, we have the choice between life and death. Ignatius thereafter always chose life. This was his art of discernment in the midst of the complexities and practicalities of everyday life and administration. And in the spirit of Paul's letter to the Corinthians, everything he did was done 'for the glory of God'. He was always beavering away at himself, working to become interiorly free, truly indifferent, just as Jesus said to the crowds: 'none of you can be my disciple unless he gives up all his possessions'. He was always on about interior freedom, stripping away any disordered affections. He was not interested in happiness except as a manifestation of that freedom and as a response to the Lord's call. While working for this deep interior freedom and indifference, he was ever attentive to the practicalities of the moment, being ever prudent. He was not one to build the tower unless he had first sat down and worked out the cost to see if he had enough to complete it. In fact our resident Jesuit historian Peter L'Estrange tells us that 8,000 of Ignatius's 10,000 letters sent from his desk in Rome related to finances and the practical preconditions for going ahead with any project. Ignatius was like the king of the gospels going to war. He would not join forces against his enemy until he had first made the calculations that he could win. He combined discernment and down to earth practical prudential decision making.

Reflecting on Ignatius in twenty-first century Australia in the light of these scripture readings, I wonder about three things: the nature of contemporary leadership; how to be true to Ignatius's vision and rules for thinking with the Church; and how to be truly discerning. I will share a word about all three.

Ignatius was one of history's great leaders when he founded the Jesuits. His detailed Constitutions for the Jesuits set out the need for the Order's leader and the criteria for the leader's choice. The leader was chosen 'to attend to the universal good' holding charge of the whole body, with the duty of 'good government, preservation and development of the whole body'. Ignatius listed many qualities for the leader, including that the leader: 'be a person whose example in the practice of all virtues is a help to others'; 'be independent of all passions'; 'know how to mingle rectitude and necessary severity with kindness and gentleness'; have 'magnanimity and fortitude' 'to bear the weakness of many'; 'be endowed with great understanding and judgment'; and 'be vigilant and solicitous.'[1] Not only Church and State, but also humanity and the planet, will suffer in the future without such leadership. God knows we need it. Let's pray for it, and let's do something about it.

I am one of those Jesuits who sometimes has been perceived as not being sufficiently loyal to the Church hierarchy. From time to time, people of good will have urged me to consider Ignatius's rules for thinking with the Church which are appended to his Spiritual Exercises. The stereotypical view of those rules is often summed up by quoting the first sentence of the 13th rule: 'To keep ourselves right in all things, we ought to hold fast to this principle: What I see as white, I would believe to be black if the hierarchical Church would thus determine it.' But life was not ever that simple, even in the time of Ignatius. He lived at a time of great theological controversy about the relationship between faith and works, and between grace and free will. Guess what? He did not take sides. He saw some validity in all points of view. The nuance of his mind and the practicality of his pastoral approach are summed up in his more rarely quoted 16th and 17th rules:

---

1. George Ganns, *The Constitutions of the Society of Jesus*, (St Loius: The Institute of Jesuit Sources, 1970), [723]-[735], 309–11.

> 16. In the same way we should notice with caution that by speaking much and emphatically of faith, without a distinction and explanation, we may give the people an occasion for growing listless and lazy in their works, either before or after these have been informed with charity.
>
> 17. Similarly, we ought not to speak so lengthily and emphatically about grace that we generate a poison harmful to liberty. Hence one may speak about faith and grace, as far as possible with God's help, for the greater praise of his divine majesty, but not in such ways or manners, especially in times as dangerous as our own, that works and free will are impaired or thought valueless.

He saw no place for faith without good works, and no place for grace without the exercise of free will. He was not focused on dogma or pedagogy. He was a pastoral priest anxious to encourage persons of high and low station to exercise discernment in their professional and personal lives. And that brings me to the third topic: discernment.

Pope Francis, the first Jesuit pope, was asked by the Jesuit magazines soon after his election as pope: What does it mean for you to be a Jesuit and pope? He spoke about the Ignatian gift of discernment:

> I was always struck by a saying that describes the vision of Ignatius: *non coerceri a maximo, sed contineri a minimo divinum est* ('not to be limited by the greatest and yet to be contained in the tiniest—this is the divine'). I thought a lot about this phrase in connection with the issue of different roles in the government of the church, about becoming the superior of somebody else: it is important not to be restricted by a larger space, and it is important to be able to stay in restricted spaces. This virtue of the large and small is magnanimity.
>
> Thanks to magnanimity, we can always look at the horizon from the position where we are. That means being able to do the little things of every day with a big

> heart open to God and to others. That means being able to appreciate the small things inside large horizons, those of the kingdom of God.[2]

For me, this is what the Ignatian vision is about at this moment in the history of the Church and in the history of Australia. We need to be able to attend to the little things but with a grandness of vision, focused on the large horizons, 'those of the kingdom of God'. We need to have an appetite for the big things, but with attention to the little things along the way, being especially attentive to the little people, the poor and marginalised who are so often left behind when bold visions are espoused, with or without theological trimmings. Pope Francis has continued to put a spring in our step by doing this, most recently with his encyclical *Laudato Si'*.

Consider just this observation from the encyclical:

> If we acknowledge the value and the fragility of nature and, at the same time, our God-given abilities, we can finally leave behind the modern myth of unlimited material progress. A fragile world, entrusted by God to human care, challenges us to devise intelligent ways of directing, developing and limiting our power.[3]

Francis has given us such licence to celebrate and enact our interior freedom, committing ourselves to a better world reflecting so many aspects of the Kingdom to come. To those who question Francis's grasp on science, economics or politics, we urge a consideration of Ignatius's 16th and 17th rules. We thank God that we are part of a discerning Church community led by such a pope at this time. We commit ourselves afresh to choosing life, to acting for the glory of God, and to discerning the greater good in the midst of the minutiae of our lives, the failings of our church hierarchy, and the vapidity of our national politics—all set against the vast horizon of the Kingdom to come and of the planet crying out for healing.

---

2. Pope Francis, 'A Big Heart Open to God', in *America*, 30 September (2013): 17.
3. Pope Francis, *Laudato Si'*, #78.

3

Getting the Structures and Processes Right

In February 2015, the Royal Commission into Institutional Responses to Child Sexual Abuse published two contrasting case studies relating to the Catholic Church and its failure adequately to protect children. Understandably the media focused on the appropriately damning findings made by the royal commission against Cardinal George Pell in his ruthless and somewhat disorganised conduct of the *Ellis* case.

In Case Study 8, the royal commission reviewed the Church's application of the *Towards Healing* Protocol to the complaint by John Ellis that he had been serially abused as a child over a five year period by Fr Aidan Duggan who was suffering dementia by the time Ellis brought his complaint. The commission found that the Archdiocese of Sydney failed to follow the protocol. Later the archdiocese conducted a review of its use of the protocol and identified a number of shortcomings in the internal church procedures. The archdiocese then appointed two senior counsel and a respected Catholic layman (Gerald Gleeson AC) to conduct a review of the review. The Gleeson panel agreed that Ellis had been denied justice and transparency and that he deserved an apology. By the time the Gleeson panel reported, Ellis had commenced litigation against the archdiocese in the Supreme Court of New South Wales claiming significant damages. Declining the services of the usual solicitors who dealt with these matters for the Church, the archdiocese retained Corrs Chambers Westgarth, a solicitors' firm which had provided services to Archbishop Pell when he was Archbishop of Melbourne. Corrs and the archbishop decided that they would fight the case hard and with significant legal armoury, incurring costs greatly in excess of what was usual for the church and its insurer Catholic Church Insurances. They retained senior counsel from the Sydney Bar.

The *Ellis* case came to public prominence because the archdiocese and their lawyers decided to play hardball in the litigation, first by pleading that there was no relevant church entity which could be sued, and second by contesting that Ellis had actually been abused by Duggan even though the relevant church authority had accepted that Ellis had been serially abused over some years. The royal commission decided to investigate this case in part as an exemplar of litigation going wrong, causing further trauma for a victim of abuse. The commission was interested in assessing:

- the relationship between litigation and institution-based redress schemes
- the experience of civil litigation by a victim of child sexual abuse
- the response of an institution that had not adopted guidelines for responding to civil litigation.[1]

Strangely, the commission decided not to include the Church's barristers in its inquiries. This made it difficult to assess where fault lay for the escalation of the confrontation in the litigation, including the subjecting of Ellis to four days of cross examination, including detailed questioning about his private life and claims of abuse. Though it is rare for a royal commission to investigate the behaviour of barristers in litigation, this commission a short time later did conduct an investigation into the conduct of the barristers who had the carriage of the prosecution of a well known swimming coach suspected of child sexual abuse while he was employed by Swimming Australia. The commission even went to great lengths to cross examine New South Wales barristers from the NSW Director of Public Prosecutions Office (including the high profile Margaret Cunneen SC) who had provided a second opinion to their Queensland counterparts as to whether prosecution was warranted. In hindsight, the commission should have called the barristers in the *Ellis* case to give evidence so as to provide the public with a better understanding

---

1. Royal Commission into Institutional Responses to Child Sexual Abuse, Report of Case Study No 8, 3.

of acceptable behaviour and tactics in hard fought litigation involving claims by a survivor of child sexual abuse.

It is one thing for a well resourced church to defend robustly a claim for compensation from (say) a major building contractor. The church, like any litigant, is entitled to play hard in court, but according to the rules, especially if the opponent is also playing hard. It is another matter when the other party justifiably claims and is believed to be a traumatised survivor of child sexual abuse.

Having found that the Archdiocese of Sydney fundamentally failed Mr Ellis in its conduct of the *Towards Healing* process, the commission found that Cardinal Pell accepted the advice of his lawyers to defend vigorously the claim brought by Mr Ellis, in part to discourage other prospective plaintiffs from litigating claims of child sexual abuse against the Church. The commission also made a formal finding that the archdiocese, the trustees and the archbishop, 'did not act fairly from a Christian point of view in the conduct of the litigation against Mr Ellis'[2]. The commission found the Sydney Archdiocese failed to conduct the litigation with Mr Ellis in a manner that adequately took account of his pastoral and other needs as a victim of sexual abuse.

It was heartening to see that the royal commission moving from Sydney to Toowoomba made no adverse findings against Bishop William Morris. In fact, the commission was quite complimentary to Morris. In the diocese of Toowoomba, there had been a long time teacher at a Catholic primary school who was a serial abuser. The protections put in place by the diocese, the Catholic Education Office and the school did not work effectively, in part because the school principal failed to discharge his obligations on receipt of a complaint of abuse from a parent, and in part because officials in the Catholic Education Office were lax in responding to complaints. Once the matter was brought to the attention of Bishop Morris he acted promptly putting the interests of students and their parents first. He sacked the incompetent staff and he set about putting in place procedures to put right the errors that had been made. The commission's key finding in relation to Morris was:

---

2. Royal Commission into Institutional Responses to Child Sexual Abuse, Case Study 8, 17, Finding 33.

That on being advised of Mr Byrnes's offending and the response of the school and the Toowoomba Catholic Education Office to the September 2007 allegations of child sexual abuse, Bishop Morris responded appropriately by:

- commissioning an independent investigation into what occurred and seeking advice and recommendations as to any actions that needed to be taken to better protect children
- appointing an independent mediator [retired High Court judge Ian Callinan] to assess and give advice as to reparation to victims and their families
- establishing a Child Abuse Response Team to develop and oversee both the pastoral and professional response and to give advice to the Diocese about improvements to child protection.[3]

Bishop Morris 'asked Mr Callinan to assist in ensuring that each victim received fair compensation for what had happened to them'. Bishop Morris 'felt that it was important that the matter be dealt with quickly and fairly so as to avoid any further suffering which might be caused by a lengthy and difficult legal process'.[4]

These contrasting findings highlight what a difference a pastorally sensitive bishop can make when he puts to one side concerns about maintaining the church patrimony and puts the well being of abused children first. The findings also highlight the tragedy that such a pastoral bishop and decent man as William Morris could be sacked by Pope Benedict XVI for failing in his duties as a bishop. When Morris was to be sacked, he had asked the papal nuncio to delay his removal until he was able to resolve all outstanding issues in relation to these incidents of abuse at his school. The Vatican declined, thereby leaving the diocese without a bishop during critical months when these matters were unresolved.

We Catholics need to admit that we are part of an institution which has continued to put the interests of victims so low in the hierarchy of concerns that Morris was not to be given a few extra months grace to resolve a difficult mediation for victims in his diocese. Vatican curial officials thought it desirable that the diocese be left anencephalic at the

---

3. Royal Commission into Institutional Responses to Child Sexual Abuse, Report of Case Study No. 6, 8, Finding 14.
4. Royal Commission into Institutional Responses to Child Sexual Abuse, Case Study 6, 44.

critical time so that another point could be made about the Vatican's enforcement against a pastorally wayward though theologically orthodox bishop. The royal commission thought it relevant to report on Morris's 'retirement' as bishop. It reported:

> On 2 May 2011, Bishop Morris retired from the position of Bishop of the Toowoomba Diocese. The circumstances of Bishop Morris's retirement were unrelated to the offences committed by Mr Byrnes and the failure of Mr Hayes and others within the TCEO to report allegations of sexual abuse made by KH or KA in September 2007. Bishop Morris retired at the request of Pope Benedict XVI following pastoral initiatives that were criticised by the Vatican as being non-compliant with Catholic Church teachings and doctrine.[5]

We have never been given a coherent rationale for Pope Benedict's sacking of Morris. After Morris had met with three investigating cardinals in Rome back in January 2008, Cardinal Re, the cardinal chairing the investigation, wrote:

> Bishop Morris is a person of integrity in morals, a man of good will and other gifts. He can continue to do much good, but the right role for him is not that of Diocesan Bishop of Toowoomba.
>
> He should be given another assignment, with special duties. With this in mind, the Holy Father asks the Metropolitan Archbishop of Brisbane and the President of the ACBC to help find the most appropriate responsibility in which Bishop Morris can continue to effectively serve the Church elsewhere in Australia, while obviously being assured of financial security for a suitable living.[6]

When Morris was sacked, Cardinal Pell had explained to an American Catholic News Agency that 'the diocese was divided quite badly and the bishop hasn't demonstrated that he's a team player'[7]. The royal

---

5. Royal Commission into Institutional Responses to Child Sexual Abuse, Case Study 6, 46.
6. Cardinal Re's notes of meeting, 19 January 2008, in William Morris, *Benedict, Me and the Cardinals Three* (Adelaide: ATF Press, 2014), 351.
7. Cardinal George Pell, Interview, Catholic News Agency, 28 May 2011, at

commission's case study on Toowoomba shows just what a fine team player Morris actually was.

On the other hand the commission's case study on Sydney provides evidence of a fairly disorganised team led by His Eminence. The report reveals a considerable disconnect even between Cardinal Pell and his Vicar General/Chancellor Monsignor Brian Rayner. There was confusion whether Rayner had kept Pell informed of the Archdiocese's formal dealings with Ellis. In his statement to the royal commission, Cardinal Pell had said, 'To the best of my recollection, I was not made aware at the time of any of those figures or offers. I was not consulted, as best I recall, about what financial amount should be considered. Nor was I made aware of the other factors which appear to have been significant in the way the facilitation process developed'.[8] The commission accepted 'that Cardinal Pell does not have a current recollection of those matters'[9]. The commission reports:

> Much of Monsignor Rayner's evidence concerned his usual practice. However, he gave evidence that he did tell the Archbishop the results of the facilitation and the amount put forward by Mr Ellis. We accept that Monsignor Rayner was a truthful witness who did his best to provide an honest account.
>
> We do not accept the submission put by the Church parties that Monsignor Rayner's evidence 'was substantially a reconstruction and would not be accepted in the absence of any corroboration from another witness or documentary evidence'.
>
> We find it compelling that, by the time Mr Ellis's solicitors had foreshadowed legal action, the Cardinal knew that amounts of money would have been discussed as part of the facilitation and that no agreement had been reached. As set out above, the Cardinal agreed he had an acute concern that people who had survived abuse by clergy would be justly dealt with. It seems unlikely that, in light of the legal

---

http://www.catholicnewsagency.com/news/cardinal-pell-says-bishop-morris-sacking-a-tragedy-but-also-a-useful-clarification/ (Accessed 13 February 2015).
8. Royal Commission into Institutional Responses to Child Sexual Abuse, Report of Case Study No. 8, 57.
9. Royal Commission into Institutional Responses to Child Sexual Abuse, Case Study 8. Finding 12, 68.

action being foreshadowed, the Cardinal, as responsible for the finances of the Archdiocese and as the Church Authority responsible for ensuring that victims were dealt with justly, would not have sought or been provided with the offers made as part of the facilitation and the outcome.[10]

The Sydney curia was not a smooth running team. Even though Cardinal Pell had appointed Monsignor Rayner to represent the Church in its dealings with Ellis and even though he knew that Rayner believed that Ellis had been abused by Duggan, he was willing to have his lawyers vigorously defend the claim by Ellis and not admit the fact that abuse had occurred. He saw no need to change his instructions to the lawyers even after receiving word that another victim of Duggan had come forward to the Church. This is the undisputed recounting of the matter by Ellis in his evidence to the royal commission:

> During the first week of the hearing, I was cross-examined over two hearing days by Senior Counsel for the Trustees and Cardinal Pell. That cross-examination included questions on 27 July 2005 as to whether my allegations were true and whether the abuse I described had happened. This line of questioning was extremely distressing for me, because I had understood until then that those instructing the lawyers for the Trustees and Cardinal Pell believed without a doubt that the abuse had happened. However, Senior Counsel clearly had different express instructions. I was saddened by the fact that the occurrence of the abuse was disputed, as I had accepted the acknowledgment of Monsignor Rayner and others as having been genuine, and now it appeared not only that Monsignor Rayner did not believe me, but that the Cardinal did not believe me either, despite what I had been led to understand by what was said by Monsignor Rayner at the facilitation. I could not fathom this in light of the assessment report.[11]

The case was then adjourned for a couple of months. Ellis was back in the witness box for more, even though by this time the Archdiocese

---

10. Royal Commission into Institutional Responses to Child Sexual Abuse, Case Study 8, 63.
11. Transcript, Royal Commission into Institutional Responses to Child Sexual Abuse, Day 53, 11 March 2014, 5415–6.

had been informed that another victim of Duggan had come forward. Ellis told the commission:

> When the hearing resumed in October 2005, I was again cross-examined over a further two days by a different barrister for the Trustees and Cardinal Pell. At the end of that hearing, detailed submissions were made by the barristers for the Trustees and Cardinal Pell questioning my credit. The submissions suggested that I was guarded and evasive and that my evidence was 'incredible'. The inference was that I had been dishonest in my testimony. This was extraordinarily upsetting and distressing, as I knew those submissions were unfair and incorrect. I had given evidence honestly to the best of my ability under considerable emotional strain.[12]

Four days of cross examination in these circumstances was outrageous. It re-traumatised Ellis. The Church's instructing solicitor, John Dalzell who knew the history of the Church's dealings with Ellis, had sat in court during the cross examination. He sent an email to the Church's barristers Stephen Rushton SC and Richard McHugh on 28 July 2005 (the day after they had cross examined Ellis as to whether his allegations were true and whether the abuse he described had happened) saying, 'Firstly thank you for all your hard work this week, it was greatly appreciated and you will be greeted with open arms at the Pearly Gates.'[13] At the royal commission Dalzell admitted that he knew the Church appointed assessor Mr Eccleston in the *Towards Healing* process had dealt directly with Ellis, believed that he had been abused and 'made an assessment that Mr Ellis was telling the truth'. When asked how he could sit behind counsel while the prying cross examination of Ellis went on putting Ellis to proof as to whether any abuse occurred, Dalzell replied:

> Your Honour, from memory—and it's been a while since I've looked at this—Mr Eccleston was appointed as an assessor to interview Mr Ellis and prepare a report. The church defendants had a discretion as to whether they accepted the report or not. I can't remember the reason, but I do remember

---

12. Transcript, Royal Commission into Institutional Responses to Child Sexual Abuse, Day 53, 5416.
13. Royal Commission into Institutional Responses to Child Sexual Abuse, Case Study 8, Exhibit 8-2, Tab 271, DUG.080.039.0541_R.

> being instructed that the report wasn't accepted and that the defence was conducted according to those instructions.[14]

Meanwhile the archdiocese had accepted the suggestion of Corrs that the archdiocese should not accept the recommendations of the Gleeson panel about how to proceed in light of the miscarrying of the *Towards Healing* process. Neither should it simply object to the panel's recommendations or refuse to implement them as this would be 'likely to reflect poorly on the Archdiocese should the Report ever come before the Court in the Ellis proceedings or otherwise become public'. Rather Corrs advised the archdiocese that the appropriate course was to 'remit the report to the panel'.[15] So all attempts to learn from and put right mistakes in the application of *Towards Healing* were put on hold for the sake of the litigation which was aimed at ensuring that no one would dare take on the church in court again.

After the trial, the matter was taken on appeal to the NSW Court of Appeal. The Archdiocese won the appeal with the court deciding that a victim could not sue the trustees. Then followed the Sydney Archdiocese's briefing to the other Australian bishops about the litigation and the church's strategy. Corrs prepared a memorandum which was circulated to the bishops. The memorandum triumphantly noted:

> The decision places a number of significant obstacles that will need to be addressed by any claimant seeking to resolve claims litigiously rather than through *Towards Healing*. Refocusing the resolution of these claims through *Towards Healing* has alone been a significant and favourable outcome of this litigation at the very least. Finally, as this decision has provided significant protection to the Cardinal and the Trustees, this in turn will give rise to a significant reduction in damages exposure and therefore the risks that are presently insured against.[16]

The memorandum falsely claimed that 'the factual allegations in this case were never challenged and, indeed for the purposes of the

---

14. Transcript, Royal Commission into Institutional Responses to Child Sexual Abuse, Day 58, 20 March 2014, 6015.
15. Royal Commission into Institutional Responses to Child Sexual Abuse, Report of Case Study 8, 68.
16. Royal Commission into Institutional Responses to Child Sexual Abuse, Report of Case Study 8, 95.

proceedings, it was conceded that the plaintiff had been exposed to the abuse as alleged.[17] Before the royal commission, Cardinal Pell and his key curial officers agreed this was plainly wrong. They had simply not adverted to the error before transmitting the communication to the other Australian bishops.

To give Cardinal Pell his due, he did in the end apologise to Mr Ellis. Just before leaving the witness box at the royal commission, Pell said:

> As former archbishop and speaking personally, I would want to say to Mr Ellis that we failed in many ways, some ways inadvertently, in our moral and pastoral responsibilities to him. I want to acknowledge his suffering and the impact of this terrible affair on his life. As the then archbishop, I have to take ultimate responsibility, and this I do. At the end of this grueling appearance for both of us at this Royal Commission, I want publicly to say sorry to him for the hurt caused him by the mistakes made and admitted by me and some of my archdiocesan personnel during the course of the *Towards Healing* process and litigation.[18]

After receipt of such a critical report from the royal commission, it would be advisable for the relevant church body (through an appropriately authorised and senior member) to scrutinise the royal commission report, indicating which findings it accepts and which findings it would join issue with, and then outlining the changes to procedures and practices in light of the accepted findings. Those materials should then be sent to the Church's Truth Justice and Healing Council to assist with a more co-ordinated whole of Church response. It is gratifying that Archbishop Fisher and the Archdiocese adopted this course of action on 14 September 2015.[19]

---

17. Royal Commission into Institutional Responses to Child Sexual Abuse, Report of Case Study 8, 96.
18. Transcript, Royal Commission into Institutional Responses to Child Sexual Abuse, 27 March 2014, Day 63, 6705.
19. The Royal Commission published its report on 11 February 2015. On 14 September 2015, the Archdiocese of Sydney published its response to each of the findings by the Royal Commission. See http://www.sydneycatholic.org/justice/royalcommission/ResponsebytheArchdioceseofSydneytotheEllisCaseStudyfindings.asp. The Archdiocese basically accepted all findings and adverse criticisms.

The royal commission has sensibly suggested that churches, like the Commonwealth Government, consider adopting a model litigant policy. The commission is considering 'the issue of model litigant codes and the principles that might guide responses to litigation by victims of child sexual abuse in an institutional context'.[20] A model litigant would never permit their counsel to impugn the credibility of a traumatised witness knowing and having communicated acceptance that what the witness has sworn is substantially true or irrefutable.

In most cases, churches like other employers and service providers are unlikely under present Australian law as developed by the High Court of Australia to be civilly liable for the criminal abuse committed by their workers provided the workers have been properly supervised at all times. To date in Australia, the victims of sexual abuse have been unlikely to succeed in court against anyone but the perpetrator or against a callously negligent employer or supervisor who had little regard for the signs that there may be a sexual predator in their midst. There have been many hurdles for a victim wanting to sue anyone but the criminal perpetrator. These hurdles may well be removed or at least substantially lowered the next time the High Court needs to consider the matter. They have been lowered or abolished in Canada and the United Kingdom.

A victim faces one additional hurdle when suing for abuse by a priest or other church personnel whose 'employer' or equivalent is a bishop or religious superior. Often as in the *Ellis* case, the alleged abuse will have occurred many years ago and now there is a new

---

Specifically, the Archdiocese 'accepts that in circumstances where Monsignor Rayner believed Mr Ellis, it should not have disputed the fact of the child sexual abuse'. Also the Archdiocese stated, 'Cardinal Pell acknowledged in his statement that the Archdiocese failed to conduct the litigation with Mr Ellis in a manner that adequately took account of his pastoral and other needs as a victim of child sexual abuse.' Also the Archdiocese stated: 'Since the Ellis litigation concluded in 2009, the Archdiocese's approach to litigation of abuse claims has also changed significantly reflecting learnings from the Ellis case and in particular that even in the context of litigation, the Archdiocese has pastoral responsibilities to victims. The Ellis Case Study Report acknowledged the submission by the Church parties that the Archdiocese's current practice is to respond to questions about the proper defendant by providing plaintiffs with information about which entity or person was responsible at the relevant time for the appointment and supervision of a person accused of sexual abuse and that damages awards will be paid through insurance or otherwise.' See http://www.sydneycatholic.org/justice/royalcommission/ArchdiocesesReviewofEllisCaseStudy.asp.

20. Royal Commission into Institutional Responses to Child Sexual Abuse, Report of Case Study 8, 119.

supervising bishop or superior. The previous bishop or superior may even have died. Who is to be sued? In the *Ellis* case, the New South Wales Court of Appeal clarified that in the case of the Catholic Church, there was no point in trying to sue the 'Trustees of the Roman Catholic Church', the statutory trust corporation that holds title to all the church lands of a diocese. That corporation may hold the assets but it does not supervise, employ or oversee clergy or other church workers. And there is no point in suing the new bishop who had nothing to do with the past abuser.

The Church should not give any appearance of hiding behind the corporate veil. Justice demands, even before the conclusion of the royal commission, that present church leaders agree to satisfy any judgment debt against their predecessors or their deceased predecessors' estates when there is an allegation of past failure to supervise or adequately investigate a sexual predator in the ranks. Any damages should be paid from church assets.

The royal commission (being appointed by the state rather than the church) had no business in finding that Cardinal Pell 'did not act fairly from a Christian point of view'[21]. The commission should stick to its brief. The finding should have been more stark: Cardinal Pell did not act fairly towards Mr Ellis. A model litigant policy should help to determine what is fair, regardless of a litigant's religious belief or commitment. The commission should leave assessments from the religious point of view to religious communities. We should maintain our proud separation of church and state.

When taking up his position as Secretary for the Economy in the Vatican, Cardinal Pell committed the church to 'substantial transparency' with Vatican finances. He said, 'We are working so that international financial standards will be followed in all the dicasteries (departments) and sections of the Holy See. Our ambition is to become . . . a model of financial management, rather than cause for occasional scandal.'[22] Transparency, professional standards and best practice should also be the hallmarks for the Church's handling of allegations of child sexual abuse within the Church. The Australian Church needs pastoral down to earth bishops like Morris who have been proved to 'get it' when it comes to dealing pastorally and professionally with child sexual abuse. His reinstatement would send a clear heartening message to all those committed to child protection.

---

21. Ibid, 17, Finding 33.
22. *The Australian*, 11 April 2015.

4

Being Inspired by our Modern Martyrs

This was the homily delivered in Canberra at the Mass celebrating the Beatification of Archbishop Oscar Romero.

It is a great joy for us the Church of Canberra to gather at the invitation of the El Salvador Australia Friendship Association to offer this mass as a Homage to the Blessed Oscar Romero and his work. We call to mind the dreadful civil war that ripped your country apart between 1979 and 1992. We recall that Oscar Romero was chosen by the Vatican to be the new archbishop of San Salvador in 1977 because he was regarded as a safe spiritual leader who was acceptable to the politically powerful in El Salvador. It was thought that he would not challenge the status quo. Such predictions came to nought given the events of 12 March 1977 when his friend, the Jesuit Fr Rutillio Grande was killed with two of his companions.

When Romero learnt about the murder of his priestly friend, the new Archbishop went to the church where the three bodies had been laid and celebrated Mass. He then spent time listening to the stories of suffering local peasant farmers. Next morning, after meeting with his priests and advisers, Romero announced that he would not attend any state occasions nor meet with the president—both traditional activities for his longtime predecessor—until Grande's death was investigated. No investigation was ever conducted, and Romero attended no state functions in his three short, but long, years as Archbishop.

The American poet Carolyn Forché who spent years in El Salvador listening to the horrific stories has often spoken in the United States about 'A Poet's Journey from El Salvador: Witness in the Light of Conscience'. She was a good friend of Romero. She was with him the week before he was assassinated in March 1980. This is how she told the story:

> I met with Monsignor in the kitchen of the convent of the Carmelite Missionary Sisters, where he told me gently that it was time for me to go home, as the situation had become too dangerous, and I was more needed in the United States, in the work of helping Americans to understand the struggle for justice. But I begged him to leave, as his was the first name on the death squads' lists. He seemed so calm that afternoon, tapping his fingers on the Bible he carried with him. I realised I was in the presence of a saint. 'No', he said, 'my place is with my people, and now your place is with yours.'

A week later on the night before he was murdered, Romero made a personal appeal to the military in a desperate attempt to stop the civilian killings in El Salvador:

> I would like to appeal in a special way to the men of the army, and in particular to the troops of the National Guard, the police and the garrisons. Brothers, you belong to our own people. You kill your own brother peasants; and in the face of an order to kill that is given by a man, the law of God that says 'Do not kill!' should prevail. No soldier is obliged to obey an order counter to the law of God. No one has to comply with an immoral law. It is time now that you recover your conscience and obey its dictates rather than the command of sin.... Therefore, in the name of God, and in the name of this long-suffering people, whose laments rise to heaven every day more tumultuous, I beseech you, I beg you, I command you! In the name of God: 'Cease the repression!'

Next day, 24 March 1980, while he was celebrating mass in a small chapel, a lone gunman came and shot him dead at the altar. Romero lay at the altar as a martyr of the Church of the Second Vatican Council. He had what Pope Francis calls 'the smell of the sheep'. He was a martyr who stood for love.

At the mass of beatification last Saturday attended by 300,000 people, eight deacons and priests carried Romero's blood-stained shirt, now a relic, to the altar in a glass case. Others decorated it with flowers and candles.

Many concelebrating priests reached out to touch the case then making the sign of the cross. Cardinal Angelo Amato, head of the Vatican's Congregation for Saints' Causes declared, 'Blessed Romero is another brilliant star that belongs to the sanctity of the church of the Americas. And thanks be to God, there are many.' So we remember too those many anonymous citizens who were gunned down during the dreadful civil war. In a message sent for the beatification, Pope Francis said Romero 'built the peace with the power of love, gave testimony of the faith with his life.'

After mass on Pentecost Sunday in Rome, Pope Francis spoke with affection about Archbishop Romero 'who was killed, out of hatred of the faith, as he celebrated the Eucharist'. Francis hailed Romero as 'a zealous pastor who, (following) in the example of Jesus, chose to be in the midst of his people, especially the poor and oppressed, even at the cost of his life.'

We recall that Romero's life and death were bookended by the Jesuit murders, first of Fr Grande in 1977 and then on 16 November 1989, of the six Jesuits, their housekeeper and her daughter at the Universidad Centroamerica (UCA). The latter killings highlighted how dirty was the civil war and how complicit was the United States. I have recently returned from Boston College whose legendary president Fr Donald Monan SJ, accompanied by other Jesuit university presidents from the USA, went to El Salvador and sat through the trial of the soldiers indicted with those killings. He spent years lobbying US congressmen to withdraw support for the unaccountable military in El Salvador, observing, 'The intellectual architects of this crime have never been publicly identified' or called to account.

Fr Ignacio Ellacuria SJ, the rector of UCA who was the main target of the later assassinations taught the American poet Forché that 'each moment of our life shapes the whole of our life, and that we are not always responsible for what befalls us but we are certainly responsible for our response'. When Ellacuria became rector of UCA he said that his country was 'an unjust and irrational reality that should be transformed' and that the university needed to contribute to social change: 'It does this in a university manner and with a Christian inspiration.' When Monan returned from El Salvador, he was fond of telling his American students: 'We must do all we can to ensure that freedom predominates over oppression, justice over injustice, truth over falsehood, and love over hatred.'

Carlos Dada writing in this week's issue of the *New Yorker* says:

> Romero was not a theologian and never considered himself part of Liberation Theology, the most radical Catholic movement born of Vatican II. But he shared with the liberationists a vision of a Gospel meant to protect the poor.

Romero was fond of asking, 'Between the powerful and the wealthy, and the poor and vulnerable, who should a pastor side with?' He had no hesitation in answering, 'I have no doubts. A pastor should stay with his people.' Carlos Dada says this 'was a political decision, but justified theologically. All of his writings include extensive biblical references, Church documents, and Papal quotations to support his assertions.'

The US bishop Ken Untener when reflecting on the life of his fellow bishop Romero wrote: 'We are workers, not master builders, ministers, not messiahs. We are prophets of a future not our own.' As we come to the table of the Eucharist, celebrating the one whose blood was poured out for us, the one who is the bread of life, let's recall the sacramental irony that the newly Blessed one in his last homily delivered minutes before his death at the altar reflected on Jesus' words in John's Gospel: 'Unless the grain of wheat falls to the ground and dies it remains alone. But if it dies it produces much fruit.' We Australians pray in thanks for those of you from El Salvador who fled to these shores to escape the terror of that dreadful civil war, and we pray that your commitment to peace and reconciliation for all continues to be one of the great fruits of the one we celebrate this evening. Let's join with Pope Francis who prayed this week, 'May those who have Archbishop Romero as a friend of faith, those who invoke him as protector and intercessor, those who admire his image, find in him the strength and courage to build the Kingdom of God, to commit to a more equal and dignified social order.'

5

Looking to Our Local Prophets

---

a. A reflection on Fr Ted Kennedy, longtime parish priest of Redfern, Sydney, on the tenth anniversary of his death

Thank you for the privilege of being your preacher this morning here at St Vincent's Redfern as we come together on Pentecost Sunday to honour the memory of our beloved Fr Ted Kennedy who died ten years ago. I first came here to Redfern in 1976 as an impressionable young Jesuit novice. I was Mum Shirl's driver. I learnt a lot behind that wheel visiting every court and prison in the region.

I am wearing my ordination vestment which was made by my mother and designed by Miriam Rose Ungunmerr, the Aboriginal artist from Nauiyu Nambiyu by the Daly River in the Northern Territory. Ted wore this vestment at Mum Shirl's funeral, and Bishop David Cremin wore it at Ted's. I have just returned from Boston where I spent a very snowy winter. On return I went fairly directly to Daly River because I have dedicated my latest book on constitutional recognition of Indigenous Australians to Miriam Rose's nephew who tragically took his own life six years ago. I went to present the book to his family. Most of you never knew him, but most of you will remember his baby face. He was the baby held by Pope John Paul II when he met with Aborigines and Torres Strait Islanders in Alice Springs in 1986. Sadly that boy felt there was no one to hold him later in life. He found no place of belonging, no foothold in either the Dreaming or the Market.

After Ted had suffered his crippling stroke, he wrote his reflection *Who is Worthy?* He wrote about 'the decision to live the rest of my life as if I were already dead. I am now more inclined to state things as they are, or as I see them, without fear or compromise.' This Pentecost Sunday, he would want all of us to incarnate the same Spirit—the spirit of truth and the spirit of courage.

I was reflecting on the prayers of the faithful composed by His Honour Chris Geraghty for Ted's funeral. In those prayers, Chris described Ted as 'a pebble in the comfortable boot of the establishment, a man who spilt his guts for others'. Contemplating the Abbott Cabinet with its five Jesuit alumni, I daresay that Ted would have been an even larger pebble in this even more comfortable boot that finds an easy fit between Catholic social teaching and the demands of modern politics.

Ten years on, there are many things which are very different from Ted's day. Some of these things even he would have found unimaginable. But he would have spoken of them without fear or compromise. Consider just a handful of those changes: a pope from the South who simply asks, 'Who am I to judge?'; a 62% vote of the Irish people in favouring of expanding the definition of civil marriage; the long awaited beatification of Oscar Romero whose identification with the poor did not win immediate Vatican approval; the call by civic leaders for an Australian cardinal to return home and answer questions posed by a royal commission; and the election of a black US president who could stand on the Selma bridge 50 years after Martin Luther King reminding the American people that Ferguson was not just an isolated incident, but neither was such killing any longer endemic nor sanctioned by law or custom. That president was able to remind the whole world that the march is not yet over:—'consciences can be stirred, and consensus can be built'.

Back home here in Australia, Ted would not have tired of reminding us that the indigenous imprisonment rates are now even higher than they were at the time of the royal commission into Aboriginal deaths in custody—twelve times the national average, with the rate for indigenous juveniles now sitting at 24 times the national average. Ted would have sounded a note of languid despair that we are still asking if or how constitutional recognition of Indigenous Australians might be achieved, rather than simply asking when.

Amidst all the change, Ted would have remained constant opening this Church to the streets of Redfern, providing a sanctuary for all on the streets, and feeding the Eucharist at all hours to those who come to watch and pray. Like the disciples and their listeners in the Acts of the Apostles, we can proclaim the message of hope in such a way that everyone who gathers can hear in their own tongues of the mighty acts of God. Gathered as we are, we look around and behold different gifts, different service, and different workings—but always the same Spirit. With Ted and Shirl, we join in the prayer of today's Sequence:

> Come, Father of the poor!
> Come, source of all our store!
> Come, within our bosoms shine.

Like them we are assured 'Solace in the midst of woe'. The Pentecost gift of the Spirit is not a cleanser to wipe away woe from our hearts or from our world. It is rather a tonic to provide solace in the midst of woe, even those woes of intractable social injustice and institutional decay.

In the words of Chris Geraghty's funeral prayers, we pray that the Father might 'soften hearts, strengthen backs, and let blood flow again in veins so that your oppressed poor may inherit the earth and have a share in its wealth'. We know that we continue to be locked up for fear of others and out of fear of those who are other. Jesus this day conveys the Spirit's gift of peace here and now. We are sent from here into the world. We are commissioned to forgive those who seek mercy and to retain the sins of those who deny justice to others. We pray for the Spirit in our hearts so that we might emulate Ted's decision to tell it as it is without fear or compromise, extending this commitment even to kindly bids to protect ourselves from our own uncircumspect selves. Filled with the Spirit, may we leave this Church fearless, unconcerned for ourselves, stirring consciences, building consensus and offering solace to all in the midst of woe.

b. A Tribute to Vicki Clark after her twenty-five years of dedicated service, leadership and achievements at the Aboriginal Catholic Ministry, Melbourne

At the conclusion of the mass held at St Pauls Outside the Walls in Rome the day after the canonisation of Mary MacKillop, Vicki Clark and a few of her Aboriginal companions invited those gathered around them to join them outside the entrance to the church. They had visited the church the previous day, concluding their researches and ascertaining the burial place of Francis Xavier Conaci. They led us in the most moving prayer for Francis, the Aboriginal boy who left Western Australia on 9 January 1849 for training as a Benedictine monk. Francis died on 17 September 1853 aged about thirteen and he lies buried outside the front of the basilica of St Paul's Outside the Walls. Gathered around his burial place, we were moved to tears. The didgeridoo was played; a traditional dance was performed; Graeme Mundine and Elsie Heiss led the prayers; and Vicki led the singing of 'The Old Wooden Cross' (the hymn which is sung at most Aboriginal funerals) and the Aboriginal Our Father. I will never forget it. It was one of the great liturgies of my life.

Little is known about Conaci other than what is found in the memoirs of Bishop Salvado who departed for Europe with two Aboriginal boys on 9 January 1849. He had come to Perth from the New Norcia mission a hundred miles away in order to sell produce there. The boys insisted on travelling with him. Salvado was then asked to travel to Europe. He reported, 'When the two boys heard of my imminent departure, they begged me to obtain permission from the Bishop for them to go with me to Europe. The Bishop was happy to meet their eager wishes, and so I got the approval of their parents and made everything ready for the voyage. On 6 January the boys were baptised by the Bishop with the names of Francis Xavier Conaci and John Baptist Dirimera'.

The boys entered the Benedictine noviceship at La Cava in Italy on 5 August 1849. Francis fell ill at La Cava, he was taken to St Paul's Outside the Walls to take the fresher air. He died there, and there he was buried.

Many of us who had arrived at St Paul's Outside the Walls knew nothing of this story. The simple Aboriginal ritual over the burial site of

Conaci was in stark contrast to the pomp and hierarchical ceremony in St Peter's Square the previous day. Vicki and her companions were there leading those of us who are the descendants of their colonisers, teaching us the history, sharing the story, and enabling us to embrace the mystery of it all in prayer. Our role was to follow, to join in prayer and to express thanks for the gracious sharing and leadership of the indigenous people.

We thank Vicki for her passionate ministry, her sense of fun in life, and her eternal hope that the Kingdom will come even for those most dispossessed and marginalised in our world. May she enjoy a great retirement. I am sure we have not heard the last of her.

Leadership of the Nation

6

The Light on the Hill

This was the Light on the Hill *Oration delivered in Bathurst in memory of Joseph Benedict Chifley in November 2013, two months after Tony Abbott defeated Kevin Rudd in the 2013 federal election.*

Many months ago, I was contacted by the Bathurst Branch of NSW Labor Party asking me to consider delivering the 2013 *Light on the Hill* Address. It was a time, as we now know from George Wright, the ALP's National Secretary, when Labor's internal polling indicated 'Labor was looking at being reduced to as few as thirty seats'. I told the organisers that usually I would despatch such an invitation to the wastepaper bin, not because I would not value the honour and the privilege to speak in remembrance of one of Australia's truly great prime ministers, but because I, a priest, would regard the invitation as too party political for consideration. On reflection, I called back, retrieving the letter from the regrets file. I was very blunt. I expressed the view that electoral wipe-out was the only conceivable outcome for the ALP and that there would be a need for the good of the country to re-found the party getting back to basic values, re-setting the political compass. I was told that was why I was being invited. So I said yes and the agreed date was 21 September 2013. Prime Minister Julia Gillard then set 14 September as the advance election date. A wake one week later seemed to be an appropriate time for reflection. Then Kevin Rudd returned to the helm and put the election date, as well as many other things, back into the mix. So the lecture was delayed until this evening so that everyone could be assured that the election would be done and dusted no matter what Kevin decided. A mate of his, I did not think he could win but that he might save the furniture. I thought he could pull off what George Wright described as a 'Dunkirk—suffering major defeat but managing to escape with . . . army intact'. Labor ended up holding fifty-five seats, living 'to fight another day'[1]. Its next generation of leaders has kept their seats in the parliament.

There have been innumerable post-mortems and words of advice as to how the party with new structures, election rules, and policies can pick itself up, dust off, and win the next election. Sadly some of those post-mortems have come with more coatings of spite and loathing. It is no part of my role in the public square as a Catholic priest to offer such advice, even if it be offered in a non-partisan, reconciling tone. I daresay it would be of little value anyway. I am neither a professional politician nor a political scientist. I am not and never have been a member of any political party. But I am a citizen who cares desperately about the health of our body politic, the contours of political morality in a pluralist democracy under the rule of law but without a bill of rights, and the values that motivate our elected leaders and that underpin the laws and policies they enact. I agree with George Wright's assessment: 'On September 7 the Australian people passed their judgment. Labor's history of infighting in office left (Labor) unworthy of re-election in too many voters' minds'.[2] For the health of the body politic, I have two fears expressed in two unanswered questions. Given the Rudd-Gillard hostility, will the Labor Party now rule a line on personal antipathies and move forward in Opposition, preparing for government? Has an Abbott Government done enough of the hard policy work and renewal in Opposition after thirteen years in government and only 6 in opposition to provide true national leadership as we face the challenges ahead?

I cannot answer those questions but hopefully I can provide some inspiration for those of all political creeds wanting to ensure a better future for our country, reflecting on the genius and toil of Joseph Benedict Chifley who led the country in times of real crisis, war and depression, and who learnt the craft of statesmanship in the cauldrons of his union as he went from striker to strike breaker, and of his political party as he went from government to losing his seat

---

1. *The Sydney Morning Herald*, 30 October 2013.
2. *The Australian*, 29 October 2013.

and leaving parliament for ten years before returning to be Treasurer and Prime Minister. Those who think the Rudd-Gillard antipathy insuperable have little knowledge of Labor in the days of Jack Lang. From the cauldron of division and antipathy emerged the great Chifley at the nation's hour of need.

At his death, Chifley was described by Dr Evatt as a 'great leader of the Australian Labour Movement; a noble Australian; a Christian statesman; fighter for the cause of social justice and the betterment of all humanity'.[3] Evatt provided this assessment of Chifley: 'He always sought unity but would never sacrifice principle to achieve the appearance of unity. He grasped essentials; he had the common touch; he was wise and supremely courageous.'[4] According to Evatt, 'Like Curtin he transcended mere party politics. John Curtin and Ben Chifley shared one noble ambition—to make Australia safe, to make Australia great.'[5] At his funeral in Bathurst, there were no eulogies. But now faithful followers gather each year in Bathurst to commemorate him with a speech. The obelisk over his grave is inscribed with his words, 'If an idea is worth fighting for, no matter the penalty, fight for the right, and truth and justice will prevail.' Gathered in the wake of a Labor defeat and a strong Coalition victory, we too for a moment want to transcend mere party politics and reflect on how we too can contribute in our distinctive ways to making Australia safer and greater. I hope my remarks will have some appeal to all members of parliament whether they be independents, members of one of the major parties, or members of one of the new parties elected to the Senate this last election.

Our Shared Debt to Aboriginal Australia

Ben Chifley's grandfather Patrick migrated here from Ireland at the age of 26. He arrived on a migrant ship, the *David McIver* in September 1858. Five years later my great great grandmother Annie and her five children including my great grandfather arrived on the very same ship. They docked not in Sydney but in Hervey Bay,

---

3. HV Evatt, 'One Line from the Poet' in NSW Branch of the Australian Labor Party, *The Light on the Hill*, (Paddington: HV Leslie, 1951), 33.
4. Evatt, *The Light on the Hill*, 34.
5. Evatt, *The Light on the Hill*, 34.

Queensland. Let me offer a brief reflection on being a descendant from Irish migrants who came here on the *David McIver* in search of a better life. In early July 2013, I was sitting alone on the shoreline at Urangan at the entrance to the vast Hervey Bay, 150 years to the day since the *David McIver* entered Hervey Bay carrying 404 immigrants, there having been only one death but also 9 births on the 107 day voyage from Liverpool.

Hervey Bay is a very expansive but shallow bay sheltered from the Pacific Ocean by the majestic Fraser Island. On 6 July 1863, the *David McIver* spent the day searching for a channel until it was anchored in 4 fathoms of water. Some of the crew then got into a small boat and made for the shore at Urangan close to where I was sitting 150 years later. They came ashore and found two Aborigines. I presume they were males. Those two Aboriginal men then without protest accompanied the crew in the boat and showed the crew the way to Captain Jeffrey's Admiralty Survey Camp. The *David McIver* was only the second migrant ship ever to come into Hervey Bay and here were two Aborigines happy to extend a helping hand to complete strangers who must have looked very strange indeed. One Aboriginal was then commissioned to send word to Maryborough 40 kilometres away. That Aboriginal walked and ran all through the night to bring word of these new arrivals. A pilot was then dispatched. Within two days, a steamer named *Queensland* arrived, towed the *David McIver* to White Cliff on Fraser Island, and then received the disembarking passengers to transport them up the Mary River to the port of Maryborough where they arrived on 9 July 1863. I know nothing more about those Aborigines who played their part in the safe arrival and settlement of my forebears. I know absolutely nothing about the Aborigines who played a part in the safe arrival and settlement of Ben Chifley's grandfather. But I do know that each of us is in their debt even 150 years later.

If my mob or Chifley's forebears were to arrive by boat today uninvited, they would be sent to Papua New Guinea. 150 years ago, the traditional owners helped my ancestors and their fellow passengers to find safe anchorage so that they might settle here permanently calling Australia home. They extended the hand of peace and welcomed the stranger. Many on the *David McIver* were eligible for land grants from the newly established Queensland Government. That was the lure for their coming to the other side of the world rather than the United States. It's a matter of some pride for me that one of Annie Brennan's great grandchildren, my father, was one of the judges who decided the 1992 *Mabo* Case finding that Aborigines had always owned the land which had been subject to those gratuitous land grants. Paul Keating then did the fabulous job of delivering the 1993 *Native Title Act*, parliament's response to the uncertainties and possibilities opened up by the High Court decision. Three years later, Labor was out of office and the High Court expanded some of the uncertainties and possibilities of native title in the *Wik* decision. The Howard government legislated its response to Keating's original Act and the High Court's more recent decision in 1998. It was a poisonous political cocktail—a 4-3 decision of the High Court being considered by an unsympathetic government and a Senate where the Catholic Tasmanian Brian Harradine had the balance of power. Keating was most displeased with Howard's tinkering with his original legislation. He was also displeased with people like Noel Pearson and me who had publicly praised Harradine for improving significantly on Howard's original position. Keating branded me the meddling priest, a label I have happily worn ever since, though I do have a preference for Kevin Rudd's more poetic descriptor. Rudd labeled me an ethical burr in the nation's saddle.

Religion, Politics and the Public Good

Paul Keating in his 2011 Lowitja O'Donoghue Oration said that the Native Title amendment law of 1998 'arose from the Coalition Government's so-called Ten Point Plan, a plan facilitated in the Senate with the support of Senator Brian Harradine under the advice of the Jesuit priest, Frank Brennan.' He then said:

> As an aside, let me say, and as a Catholic, let me say, whenever you witness the zealotry of professional Catholics in respect of indigenous issues, invariably you find indigenous interests subordinated to their personal notions of justice and equity: because unlike the rest of us, they enjoy some kind of divine guidance.[6]

---

6. PJ Keating, *Afterwords* (Melbourne: Allen and Unwin, 2011), 90.

This was reminiscent of Chifley's remark about Santamaria and the Groupers: 'one of the most dangerous individuals you could have in public life was a religious fanatic.'[7] He thought the 'religious fanatic is worse than the political fanatic'.[8] Keating was on to something when he spoke of indigenous interests and notions of justice and equity. But I don't think personal notions of justice and equity count for much in the public square of a pluralist democracy like Australia unless those notions can be rendered comprehensible and adoptable by other citizens who do not share your religious or philosophical world view. I was privileged to know Brian Harradine as a friend. He was assuredly a very canny politician. But I never knew him to claim any sort of divine guidance when making a political decision. I definitely make no such claim.

The confusion over religion and politics is presently being played out in Australia over the same sex marriage debate. I am a supporter of civil unions. Conceding that neither side of the debate is much interested in that outcome, I have concluded that we can no longer draw a line between civil unions and same sex marriage. During the 2013 federal election, Kevin Rudd pulled out all stops to advocate same sex marriage legislation in the Commonwealth Parliament. Tony Abbott stuck firmly to the line that his party would maintain party policy that marriage is a relationship between one man and one woman to the exclusion of others and that the party policy would be maintained unless and until the party revised its position, including whether or not to allow a conscience vote. In the Liberal Party, as distinct from the Labor Party, members are always free to cross the floor without the risk of automatic expulsion from the party—though their prospects of promotion tend to take a nosedive.

Any extension of the civil law's definition of marriage should be the preserve of the Commonwealth Parliament with all members being granted a conscience vote. Presently the 1961 Commonwealth *Marriage Act* as amended states that 'marriage means the union of a man and a woman to the exclusion of all others, voluntarily entered into for life'.

---

7. David Day, *Chifley*,(Melburne: Harper Collins, 2001), 477.
8. Quoted in *Australian Dictionary of Biography*, Volume 13, (Melbourne: Melbourne University Press, 1993), 419.

Under the Australian Constitution, the Commonwealth Parliament has power to make laws with respect to marriage. So too do the States. And since 1978, so too does the ACT Legislative Assembly. But if a Commonwealth law purports to cover the field, any State or Territory law does not operate to the extent of any inconsistency. Undoubtedly the Commonwealth will argue in the High Court that it has covered the field on marriage since 1961 and it should be left to do so. Advocates for 'marriage equality' frustrated by the slow pace of change at a Commonwealth level have decided to pursue state and territory legislation for forms of unequal and inferior marriage recognition in the hope of providing further political pressure for the Commonwealth to act.

Marriage equality advocates are pursuing marriage inequality at a state level in the hope of pressuring the Commonwealth into marriage equality. In the process they risk blowing apart the national coherence of marriage laws put in place in 1961. History points to the wisdom of a conscience vote in the national parliament on this issue.

Introducing the Commonwealth *Marriage Bill* on 19 May 1960, Sir Garfield Barwick indicated that he had taken a full year to prepare the legislation and he was prepared to wait many more months to debate the bill 'making with the States the several administrative arrangements which the bill contemplates'. He said: 'the measure will not be treated as a party measure and . . . members will be free to adopt their own attitudes and to express them by their vote, freely.'[9]

Gough Whitlam, Deputy Leader of the Opposition with the carriage of the matter for the Labor Party, reminded the Parliament on 17 August 1960: 'When the Attorney General (Sir Garfield Barwick) made his second reading speech on this bill, he announced that while the Government would take full responsibility for having made the proposals contained in the measure and would support them, as a government, the legislation would not be treated as a party measure, and honourable members would be free to adopt their own attitudes to it and express them freely by their votes. The Opposition has resolved to take the same course.'[10]

---

9. 1960 *Commonwealth Parliamentary Debates* 2000 (HofR); 19 May 1960.
10. 1960 *Commonwealth Parliamentary Debates* 114 (HofR); 17 August 1960.

Tony Abbott and Bill Shorten should ensure that their members have the same conscience vote available to them on same sex marriage.

Religion is much less relevant now to the civil definition of marriage because while the crude marriage rate continues to decline (from 7.3 in 1960 to 5.5 in 2008), the proportion of civil marriages continues to increase. A century ago, 95% of marriages were church marriages; in 1969, 89% of marriages were still being performed in church. By 2010, 69% of all marriages were performed by civil celebrants.

Some strong advocates of traditional marriage, including the Australian Christian Lobby, have been suggesting that the matter should be resolved by referendum. That is a bad idea. In Australia, we expect our members of parliament to make the statutory law and our judges to shape the common law and interpret the Constitution. We the people vote by referendum only to change the Constitution. Occasionally there is a case to be made for a plebiscite when we are trying to determine a particular question to put to the people by referendum to change the Constitution. This is what we did when we wanted to determine whether we were ready to vote for a particular form of republic.

Groups like the Australian Christian Lobby should be careful what they wish for. If a referendum on same sex marriage, why not a referendum on (say) the death penalty? If the opinion polls are right, there is no doubt the way that one would go. Or a referendum on excluding boat people from Australia? Or a referendum on euthanasia? There are good reasons for avoiding the populist politics of lawmaking by direct popular vote of the people.

Writing in an academic journal and reflecting on the passage of the *Marriage Act 1961*, Barwick said: 'To bring unity to the marriage law of Australia was not, however, the main task of the architects of the *Marriage Act*. Their main task was to produce a marriage code suitable to present-day Australian needs, a code which, on the one hand, paid proper regard to the antiquity and foundations of marriage as an institution, but which, on the other, resolved modern problems in a modern way.'[11] This remains our task, and it is best done by the Australian Parliament exercising a conscience vote rather than State

---

11. Garfield Barwick, 'The Commonwealth Marriage Act', *Melbourne Law Review*, 3 (1961-2): 277.

and Territory legislatures tinkering and then leaving the matter to the High Court.

As a Catholic priest and as an Australian citizen I think the public good would be best served by all parties in the federal parliament being granted a conscience vote on same sex marriage. I oppose same sex marriage laws being enacted in state and territory parliaments because they would be either inoperative or disruptive of a national code while providing an unequal form of marriage.

In August 2013 before appearing on national television to discuss same sex marriage, I did three things. I had asked the congregation at my regular Sunday mass for comment after mass and many older parishioners said that they did not want to see any discrimination against same sex couples but they were not sure that a same sex relationship was the same as their marriage. I asked a young couple whose marriage I had recently performed with a nuptial mass what they thought and they made it very clear to me that for their generation the whole discussion was a bit of a yawn and the answer for civil law was self-evident. I called a lesbian Catholic I knew who had children with her partner and she told me that she was a lesbian and always would be; that she was Catholic and always would be; that the clergy should get over this idea that they were the gatekeepers to the gospels and the sacraments because the key message was that God is love.

I think our federal politicians voting according to conscience and not according to party dictate will be well positioned to judge when the country is ready to make the change to marriage by including the unions of same sex couples. If and when they do, I will not lose any sleep over it and I will be delighted for those same sex couples who think it will help social support and endorsement of their faithful committed relationships. I will spare a thought for those older married Australians who remain unconvinced that a same sex marriage relationship is the same as theirs. I will remain vigilant that state laws and policies should not encourage the creation of children without a known biological father and known biological mother.

Leading by Conscience, not Populism

Chifley was the exemplar of making hard decisions for the public good. And that's what the trade-off between sectional interests and notions of justice and equity is all about. And it has to be done in the light of cold, hard political realities. There will be many such challenges confronting our national leaders in the next few years as they determine how to treat asylum seekers, how to reduce our reliance on carbon fuels, how to redistribute the wealth of the finite mining boom, how to extend insurance to those suffering disabilities, and how to enhance our education system. And they will do all these things with a Senate less predictable than we have seen in a very long time.

Chifley was Minister for Defence back in 1931 having entered parliament just three years earlier at the age of 43. Speaking to the *Debt Conversion Agreement Bill* on 25 June 1931, he conceded that it was a compromise unsupported even by key people in the Labor ranks. The Scullin government was besieged by Jack Lang on the left and the bankers on the right. The Senate had rejected the government's *Fiduciary Bill* in April 1931. So the government had to go back to tors and negotiate with the premiers and the banks. The options were: resign government; adopt the demands of the premiers and the banks cutting salaries and pensions in return for which government expenditure would continue to be underwritten; or default on loan repayments. Chifley told Parliament:

> The plan that is outlined in the bill has been attacked from various angles—by some honourable members for sentimental reasons, by many because they sincerely believe that it is a retrograde step, and by some, unconsciously perhaps, for reasons of self interest. I regret to have to say that the hostility of some members is inspired by the belief that the plan will be unpopular. The sentimental objectors are those who are unwilling to defer the realisation of the ideals for which they have striven in the Labour movement, and I appreciate their view. But, after all, what is the plan and from whom does it emanate? It is not the result of the thought of any one man or of any one political party ... The last conference ... included representatives of conservative opinion and the various shades of political thought within the Labour movement. There were

> Labour premiers who might be termed moderates, and one Labour Premier whom the militants, no doubt, regard as the ideal leader [Jack Lang of course]. Those men meeting in conference with their political opponents, were able to look deep into the economic and financial problems. They had the assistance of the most eminent financiers and economists in Australia, and from their study of the problem in the light of the facts and advice, more complete than are available to the Members of this House, this plan evolved. The sponsors of it do not pretend that it is entirely acceptable to them; some delegates no doubt regretted that it did not go as far as they thought it should, whilst others, possibly, feared that it went too far in certain directions. But they had to devise a method of restoring financial stability, and this represented a fair compromise to which all could subscribe.[12]

Chifley had been a minister only a few months. He had to stand on principle on a compromise in the face of opposition from near and far, including from his newfound friend in Labor, John Curtin. He took the advice of experts. He mastered the brief. He followed due political process. He honoured Cabinet solidarity. He did not descend to *ad hominem* attack. He felt the pain deeply. He told Parliament: 'I do not wish to introduce personal passion into this debate; I would prefer to give to the opponents of this plan credit for sincerity, but I might easily contrast their attitude with that of men who are taking an unpopular stand which may lead to their political extinction.'[13]

Chifley was a political realist. He was prepared to walk wide eyed off the precipice into political oblivion because no other course of action would satisfy his conscience when he tried to balance sectional interests and the common good in the scales of justice. He said:

> I do not know how the people that I represent will view my action. I know that it is popular to decry those who support the plan. Unpalatable and distasteful though it is, I am giving it my support, because I believe that if the Government fails to do something in a general way to rectify the position, national ruin is inevitable. I hope that it will be possible to modify the proposals, and to soften their severity. But the members of

---

12. 1931 *Commonwealth Parliamentary Debates* (HofR) 3062; 25 June 1931.
13. 1931 *Commonwealth Parliamentary Debates* (HofR) 3063; 25 June 1931.

Parliament are charged with a national responsibility, and their personal concerns must be temporarily set aside. I am not like the honourable member for Adelaide (Mr Yates), who airily says that he does not care what happens. I do care. I do not want to lose my seat in Parliament. I appreciate the trust placed in me by my constituents, and regard it as an honour to represent them here. I am endeavouring to do the right thing... The motive that inspires the action taken by a man counts a great deal when his conduct is judged. This plan is backed by men who have had experience in governing the country, who know the facts and who see the position clearly; but those who oppose it have nothing but hope to support their attitude.[14]

It's a long time since we have heard any such stand on principle taken by any of our politicians. And yes, it was to mean nine years in political oblivion. But then phoenix like, Chifley, bloodied and strong, was able to take on the mantle of leadership during the most critical days of World War II. Back then in 1931, he told Parliament, 'My action in this matter may mean my political extinction. Possibly it will not be justified by events to follow. However, the personal political welfare of the individual must be set aside. It is the nation that counts in a crisis such as this. If my constituents consider that I have failed, and that my action, however sincere, is wrong, I shall abide without complaint by their decision. While I am in this Parliament I must endeavour to help the country to emerge successfully from this, the greatest economic crisis in its history. My action is not the outcome of egotism, of the belief that everything that I do is right. It is taken in the belief that this plan embodies a general solution that will prevent the country from lapsing into chaos.'[15]

He concluded his *apologia pro vita sua* to Parliament with these words: 'If we, in this Parliament, can do something to prevent such a lamentable condition of affairs, we shall at least have served honestly the persons whom we are sent here to represent.'[16]

The *National Advocate* reprinted the speech in full describing it as 'sincere and statesmanlike'.[17] Back home, Chifley was running into

---

14. 1931 *Commonwealth Parliamentary Debates* (HofR) 3065; 25 June 1931.
15. 1931 *Commonwealth Parliamentary Debates* (HofR) 3065; 25 June 1931.
16. 1931 *Commonwealth Parliamentary Debates* (HofR) 3065-6; 25 June 1931.
17. *National Advocate* 3 July 1931. See David Day, *Chifley*, Harper Collins, 266-8.

trouble with his union and there were moves to expel him. He wrote to the branch chairman saying: 'I have never had any illusions about the hard road I travel but the attacks of opponents or even loss of faith by my friends will never cause me to do anything but what I believe the best possible for the people in the circumstances. My views or actions may appear wrong—they may be wrong. But they are what I sincerely believe to be right.'[18] On 4 October 1931, his union expelled him. He appealed the decision but the divisions in the union were so bad that he decided to withdraw his application on the very day that Jack Lang's leader in the federal parliament voted with the Opposition bringing down the Scullin government. At the ensuing election Chifley lost his seat by just 476 votes being besieged on two sides by the UAP and the Langite Tony Luchetti. It would be nine years before he was back again as a member of the House of Representatives. On his return, Curtin immediately made him Treasurer and a member of the War Cabinet. And Luchetti became his campaign manager.

Doing the Right Things with Justice and Compassion and the Tough Things in the National Interest

I wonder what Chifley would have done when confronted with the poisonous cocktail of the contemporary asylum issue. Would he have tried a Pacific Solution, a Timor Solution, a Malaysia Solution, or a PNG Solution? After the 12 years of angst over the issue, what would he have done from the Opposition benches today? Both sides of Australian politics are now committed to stopping the boats but disagree as to how it might best be done. The minor parties (Greens, Palmer United and DLP) have some ethical objections. The Abbott government has been elected with a strong mandate to stop the boats. For the next few months, the new government will not be much interested in public discussion about the ethics of the policy. It will be more a matter of 'whatever it takes'. If the boats do stop, it might then be opportune to commence discussion about how Australia might contribute to better processing and protection of asylum seekers upstream in Indonesia and Malaysia. If the boats do not stop, the government will need to engage the community about the ethical

---

18. Letter to Ernie Cole, quoted by Day, *Chifley*, 269.

bottom line for long term detention and banishment of refugees to countries such as Nauru and PNG. Chifley would think it time to set down a few incontrovertible ethical parameters. He would take professional advice. He would insist on a fair go for all—those on boats, those stranded in remote camps, and those trapped in transit countries. He would not take refuge in flowery rhetoric or one line slogans.

Though most of our neighbours are not signatories to the *Refugee Convention*, Australia should remain a party to the Convention, and refugee advocates should stop overstating or misstating the rights protected by the Convention and the *UN Declaration of Human Rights* (UNDHR). Article 14(1) of the UNDHR provides: 'Everyone has the right to seek and to enjoy in other countries asylum from persecution.' Back in 1948, the drafters had suggested that a person have the right to be 'granted asylum'—a legal right to just turn up here by boat! Australia was one of the strong, successful opponents, being prepared to acknowledge only the individual's right 'to seek and enjoy asylum', because such a right would not include the right to enter another country and it would not create a duty for a country to permit entry by the asylum seeker. That's why Article 31(1) of the *Refugee Convention* deals as it does with the illegal entry or presence of an asylum seeker who has entered or is present without authorisation. It provides: 'The Contracting States shall not impose penalties, on account of their illegal entry or presence, on refugees who, coming directly from a territory where their life or freedom was threatened in the sense of article 1, enter or are present in their territory without authorisation, provided they present themselves without delay to the authorities and show good cause for their illegal entry or presence.' The immunity from penalty is restricted to refugees 'coming directly from a territory where their life or freedom was threatened'. The Australian Government website is correct when it states: 'International law recognises that people at risk of persecution have a legal right to flee their country and seek refuge elsewhere, but does not give them a right to enter a country of which they are not a national. Nor do people at risk of persecution have a right to choose their preferred country of protection.' There is a right to leave your country. There is a right to re-enter your country. There is a right to seek asylum. But there is no right to enter another country of which you are not a national—even to seek asylum. Should you have succeeded in entering another country not your own, whether legally or illegally, you have a right to enjoy asylum if you are a refugee.

Chifley would concede that the moral argument is another matter. But it is important to be clear about Australia's international obligations under the UNDHR and the *Refugee Convention*. Unfortunately even the website of the Refugee Council of Australia is wrong when it states: 'The UN Refugee Convention (to which Australia is a signatory) recognises that refugees have a right to enter a country for the purposes of seeking asylum, regardless of how they arrive or whether they hold valid travel or identity documents.'[19] Given that most of our neighbours are not signatories to the *Refugee Convention*, there is no point in over-stating our legal obligations when we come to the moral arguments and the diplomatic negotiations that will be required to enhance the processing and protection of refugees in our region. It would be folly to abandon the international legal instruments and just rely on moral argument and diplomatic negotiations. We should maintain the safety net of law. The political atmosphere is such that the safety net will become so frayed as to be useless if refugee advocates continue to overstate and mis-state the law.

There is no doubt that the reforms of July 2008 instituted by the Rudd Government and not opposed by the Nelson Opposition contributed to a sharp increase in the arrival of boat people. The annual arrivals continued to spiral upwards—from 2856, to 6689, a brief drop to 4730, then up to 17,271, and then up again to 25,145. By the time Kevin Rudd had become prime minister for the second time in June 2013 the boat arrivals were running at 3,300 per month (40,000 per annum). There was intelligence available that the people smuggling networks were now so adept at plying their trade in Indonesia that the numbers could escalate even further. These increases were not related to increased global refugee flows nor to new refugee producing situations in the region. There had been at least 900 deaths at sea since the 2008 reforms were instituted. Something had to be done—not just for crass political gain but for sound ethical reasons.

Since the High Court's rejection of the Gillard government's Malaysia solution, there has been a need to consider how ethically

---

19. The website has since been corrected.

and practically to stop the boats. The lack of bipartisan agreement meant that the recommendations of the Houston panel could be only partially implemented. In the medium term, it might be possible to negotiate a regional agreement involving at least Australia, Indonesia and Malaysia. An agreement, with UNHCR backing, could provide basic protection and processing for asylum seekers transiting Malaysia and Indonesia. Asylum seekers headed for Australia could then be intercepted and promptly screened to determine that none was in direct flight from persecution in Indonesia. They could then be flown back safely to Indonesia and placed at the end of a real queue. Provided the necessary screening was done, it could then be appropriate to adopt Alexander Downer's suggestion: 'Australia would fly back to Indonesia anyone who arrived here by boat without a visa. In exchange, Australia would take, one for one, UNHCR approved refugees from refugee camps in Indonesia.'[20] Such an agreement would take many months, if not years, to negotiate and implement. Admittedly, it would not provide a short term solution to stopping the boats.

Kevin Rudd's pre-election agreements negotiated with Papua New Guinea and Nauru and first announced on 19 July 2013 were aimed at stopping the boats. It was the equivalent of a 'shock and awe' measure, threatening dreadful outcomes for people, hopefully deterring them from even considering getting on board a boat. During the 2013 election campaign, both major political parties tried to convince the electors that they would be able to design policies which stopped the boats.

During its last year in office, Labor had increased the humanitarian component of our migration program from 13,750 to 20,000 places - with 12,000 of those places being allocated to refugees offshore, 8,000 being available for refugees onshore and the special humanitarian program. The Coalition initially supported the increase but reversed this commitment during the election campaign. The Abbott Government said it would provide only 2,750 places for onshore applicants.

If adopting the key planks of the Rudd plan, the Abbott government could give the 'shock and awe' response greater ethical coherence if

---

20. *The Australian*, 30 September 2013.

they took the following seven steps. These are steps of which I think Chifley would approve.

First, Tony Abbott should continue discussions with Jakarta with an eye to a negotiated agreement with both Indonesia and Malaysia aimed at upstream improvement of processing and protection.

Second, the Abbott government should return to its previous commitment to increase the humanitarian quota to 20,000.

Third, Scott Morrison should order an ethical reassessment of the plight of those who came by boat to Australia after the Rudd announcement of 19 July 2013 without notice of the new shock and awe policy, bearing in mind that many of those who arrived immediately after 19 July had received no notice of the new policy. This was admitted by Minister Tony Burke when he told the media on 22 August 2013: 'First week after the announcement, the figures remained very high, but let's not forget those figures include people who are already at sea.'[21]

Fourth, Scott Morrison should undertake to care for unaccompanied minors who arrive in Australia's territorial waters until they can be safely resettled or safely returned to their family or to the guardians in transit from whom they were separated.

Fifth, Scott Morrison should institute safeguards, including a transparent complaints mechanism, in PNG and Nauru consistent with the safeguards recommended by the Houston Panel for both Pacific processing countries and for Malaysia under the Malaysia Solution.

Sixth, Tony Abbott should introduce a bill to Parliament this month detailing the measures aimed at stopping the boats, thereby putting beyond legal doubt the 'shock and awe measures' implemented on the eve of the election campaign without parliamentary scrutiny, and locking in the major political parties so that petty party point scoring might cease. Debate on the bill would allow both sides of the Chamber to purge themselves of the hypocrisy that has accompanied Labor's unctuous condemnation of John Howard's Pacific Solution and the Coalition's unctuous condemnation of Julia Gillard's Malaysia Solution. The bill would undoubtedly win the support of the major political parties, restoring a more bipartisan approach as existed

---

21. Tony Burke, Transcript, Press Conference, Sydney, 22 August 2013 available at <http://www.alp.org.au/cm22_220813>. Accessed 12 August 2015.

in July 2008 when Minister Chris Evans announced 'the seven key immigration values' then unanimously embraced by the Parliament's Joint Standing Committee on Migration.

Seventh, the government should commit itself to the prompt processing onshore of Papuan asylum seekers in direct flight from West Papua. The Coalition's Policy on asylum seekers published during the election campaign states, 'The Coalition will work with our regional partners to address the secondary movement of asylum seekers into our region as a transit point to illegally enter Australia through the establishment of a comprehensive Regional Deterrence Framework'. Papuans fleeing persecution at home are not engaged in secondary movement. If refugees, they are in direct flight from persecution. The Abbott government should recommit to our obligation under the *Refugee Convention* to grant asylum to refugees who have entered Australia in direct flight from persecution.

While waiting to see if the boats do stop, all Australians can consider how better to contribute to protection and processing of asylum seekers in the region.

Keeping the Light on the Hill Shining into the Dark Crevices

Those who think stopping the boats is a major national emergency have no historical sense of perspective. Those who think the Gonski educational reforms and the proposed National Disability Scheme are big reforms need to consider the leaps and bounds made with post war reconstruction. Chifley as Treasurer was Curtin's right hand man in financing the national war effort. As prime minister, he then forged the post-war reconstruction. Think just of the Snowy Mountains Scheme and the Holden motor car for starters. There were big blunders along the way including the attempted nationalisation of the banks. An opponent as wily as Robert Menzies was well able to capitalise on such mistakes. With a swing of 3.7% against it, the Chifley government lost power on 10 December 1949. The Coalition held 74 seats to Labor's 47. During that election campaign, Chifley said, 'It is the duty and the responsibility of the community, and particularly those more fortunately placed, to see that our less fortunate fellow citizens are protected from those shafts of fate which leave them helpless and without hope . . . That is the objective for which we are striving. It is . . . the beacon, the light on the hill, to which our eyes are always turned and to which our efforts are always directed.'[22] Tony Luchetti later made the claim: 'Ben got that from me originally, you know, because in our first clash in '31, I said, "The Lang plan stands as a beacon to lead men on to the path that they should travel for better times etc, etc." and that theme, that light on the hill, was accepted by Ben and Ben started to use it.'[23] I will leave it to the historians to work that one out. Suffice to say that the phrase is now identified with Chifley and not with the old Lang forces who had opposed him so vociferously for so long. No doubt, Ben Chifley had in the back of his mind the scripture verses:

> You are the light of the world. A city set on a hill cannot be hidden. Nor do people light a lamp and put it under a basket, but on a stand, and it gives light to all in the house. In the same way, let your light shine before others. (Mt 5:14–16)

As Leader of the Opposition, Chifley started running out of puff. He was not helped by Evatt deciding to appear in the Communist Party Dissolution Case. But he was not embittered. And he did not lose sight of his core values. His last major political speech was to the Labor Party Annual Conference of NSW Branch on 10 June 1951. He expressed his confidence that another war was less likely than 12 months before but that there were major challenges on the economic front nationally and internationally. He said, 'If, from time to time, the policy is not favoured by the majority of the people there is no reason why the things we fight for should be put aside to curry favour with any section of the people. I say to you that, in the period I have been leader, I have always believed that the Movement has to make up its mind what is the right thing to do and, no matter what the daily press says or any section of the community might say, we must go on

---

22. JB Chifley, 'No Glittering Promises', Election Policy Speech, 14 November 1949, in AW Stargardt, *Things Worth Fighting For: Speeches of Joseph Benedict Chifley*, (Melbourne: Melbourne University Press, 1952), 73 at 85.
23. AS Luchetti interviewed by Andrew Moore in the Parliament's Bicentenary oral history project, TRC 4900/3, Transcript, Tape 4, page 5.

fighting. I hope the spirit which animated the people who began the Labor movement goes on today.'[24]

He concluded:

> I can only hope that the sincerity which you have shown over the years in victory and defeat won't be lost; that you will be inspired by the same things which inspired the pioneers of this Movement, and that you will not be frightened and made to get over to the 'right' because of the whispered word 'Communist'. I could not be called a 'young radical' but if I think a thing is worth fighting for, no matter what the penalty is, I will fight for the right, and truth and justice will always prevail.[25]

In the 2012 *Light on the Hill* address, Bill Shorten said, 'That's what the light on the hill means to me—equal opportunity—a truly fair go.' He spoke of the remarkable Australians who keep the fire burning: 'They are my light on the hill—each and every one of them is an incandescent beacon.'[26] He actually said each of them 'are' an incandescent beacon. I must have a word to his old English teacher back there at Xavier College about that. We expect more from our Jesuit products, no matter what side of the House they are on! Chifley was more expansive in his own *Light on the Hill* address. He looked offshore, contemplating Australia's place in the world and our relative affluence and security. He said: 'Labour has fought to give the Australian people equality of opportunity and a decent standard of living. But nobody has fought in Asian countries to give the people anything of that character. That struggle has now begun . . . The Australian people cannot cure the evils in Asian countries nor, indeed, the economic evils that befall the countries of Europe —whether western or eastern Europe. All we can do is, by our own example, by such assistance as we can give, by way of advice, or by

---

24. JB Chifley, 'Be Quite Clear What You Believe in and Fight for it', Address to NSW Branch of the Australian Labor Party, 10 June 1951, in Stargardt, 385.
25. JB Chifley, 'Be Quite Clear What You Believe in and Fight for it,', 392–3.
26. Bill Shorten, 'If things are right, they will come your way', Light on the Hill Address, 22 September 2012, available at <http://billshorten.com.au/light-on-the-hill-address>. Accessed 12 August 2015.

direct financial assistance, play our own very small part in a great world which is filled with economic trouble.'[27]

On Social Justice Sunday in 2013, the Australian Churches issued statements on the need for Australia to contribute more in foreign aid and assistance particularly to our near neighbours. Both sides of politics went into the election campaign committed to cutting our aid budget. We would do well to recall Chifley's call to the New South Wales branch of the Australian Labor Party when he told the annual conference: 'I do not think that we are so narrow-minded and parochial that we want good conditions for ourselves, but are entirely indifferent to the needs of hundreds of millions of workers in the world. The Labour movement has a much wider conception than that—to help everybody in the world who is not as fortunate as we are.'[28]

Those of us schooled in the Christian tradition often contemplate the parable of the Good Samaritan, as Chifley surely did. That parable works well for one stray Jew fallen by the wayside in desperate need. It works even better when the travelling Samaritan has access to a trusting Jewish innkeeper who will offer credit on spec. It needs some imaginative discernment once you postulate hundreds fallen by the wayside, millions even more desperate in faraway places, and institutional innkeepers who have shareholders or voters to satisfy. The gospel message of charity and justice must always be prophetic, pedagogical and practical. The democratically elected leaders of a robust pluralist nation such as Australia have to accept that they cannot help everyone in need on the planet and they are elected to maintain secure borders and a standard of living for our citizens which could not be emulated for all persons on the planet. Chifley was not averse to thinking in universal terms. He said in his *Light on the Hill* address: 'I have tried to think, when facing these things, of all the people of the community and not to think of any one particular section—because if the Labour movement means anything at all it

---

27. JB Chifley, 'For the Betterment of Mankind—Anywhere', Address to NSW Branch of the Australian Labor Party, 12 June 1949, in Stargardt, 58 at 59.
28. JB Chifley, 'For the Betterment of Mankind—Anywhere', 59.

means justice to all.'[29] When speaking of the job of any Labor minister, he said, 'The job of the evangelist is never easy.'[30]

He was not just about charity nor just about tending to the isolated person in need by the side of the road. For him, politics was a more universal, evangelical calling demanding structural change. He concluded his *Light on the Hill* address:

> I try to think of the Labour movement, not as putting an extra sixpence into somebody's pocket, or making somebody Prime Minister or Premier, but as a movement bringing something better to the people, better standards of living, greater happiness to the mass of the people. We have a great objective —the light on the hill—which we aim to reach by working for the betterment of mankind not only here but anywhere we may give a helping hand. If it were not for that, the Labour movement would not be worth fighting for. If the movement can make someone more comfortable, give to some father or mother a greater feeling of security for their children, a feeling that if a depression comes there will be work, that the government is striving its hardest to do its best, then the Labour movement will be completely justified. It does not matter about persons like me who have our limitations. I only hope that the generosity, kindness and friendliness shown to me by thousands of my colleagues in the Labour movement will continue to be given to the movement and add zest to its work.[31]

Policy, politics and public morality all had their place for Chifley. He was on about much more than individual action, individual rights and non-discrimination. Rather than focusing on sectional interests, rather than invoking ideas of class warfare or gender warfare, he placed the common good, the public interest, centre stage. If leading us today, he would insist that we accommodate group rights as well as individual rights, collective action as well as individual action, and the legitimate aspirations of those who are so 'other' or so vulnerable as not to count in the political calculus or judicial reasoning. He would be at home with those citizens who both think outside the square

---

29. JB Chifley, 'For the Betterment of Mankind—Anywhere', 61.
30. JB Chifley, 'For the Betterment of Mankind—Anywhere', 65.
31. JB Chifley, 'For the Betterment of Mankind—Anywhere', 65.

of present orthodoxy in pursuit of the universalism which alone guarantees protection of those both inside and outside the square, and have the prudence to know when the square needs to be redrawn.

Speaking at the National Press Club in November 2013, George Wright, ALP National Secretary said, 'At this election the Liberals won the past. But they did not win the future.'[32] Neither did Labor. The challenge is to look to the past and to see how the future can be won through leadership which is both cunning and selfless, pragmatic and idealistic. The Abbott government announced an audit of all government programs with a stipulation that 'government should do for people what they cannot do, or cannot do efficiently, for themselves, but no more.' Chifley would ask government to do two more things: to do for people those things which guarantee their fundamental rights and entitlements and those things which enhance their capacity decently to help and co-operate with their neighbours. In other words, he would insist that the government, regardless of the efficiency of individual action, assist with the provision of a social safety net and of a social web for fostering community engagement. Chifley would urge us all to hold respectfully both to the idealism of the light on the hill and to the pragmatism of the hip-pocket nerve, each of which commanded his use, if not his original authorship. The country continues to be well-served by the leadership example of Joseph Benedict Chifley. Long may his light shine on the dark crevices of our contemporary political landscape. May the light on the hill continue to shine on the path of our common quest, motivated by public service and not the spoils of office. May we take practical steps on that path, united not divided, towards our celebrated ideal of a fair go for all. With hope and realism, may we celebrate Leonard Cohen's 'Anthem':

> Ring the bells that still can ring
> Forget your perfect offering
> There is a crack, a crack in everything
> That's how the light gets in.
> That's how the light gets in.
> That's how the light gets in.

---

32. *The Australian*, 30 October 2013.

7

The Spirit of ANZAC

This address was delivered in the Memorial Church at Harvard on the centenary of the ANZAC landing at Gallipoli, 25 April 2015.

This Memorial Church at Harvard was dedicated on Armistice Day 1932 in memory of those who died in World War I. The inscription over the south entrance to the memorial room reads, 'In grateful memory of the Harvard men who died in the World War we have built this Church.'

It is fitting that we, Australians, New Zealanders, Turks and Americans should gather in this place to mark the centenary of Anzac Day, the day on which Australians and New Zealanders landed in the stillness of the early dawn on the Turkish shoreline wanting to assist with the Allies' advance on Constantinople, now Istanbul, the day on which the Turks commenced a successful, eight month campaign to defend their homeland against the assault.

Nineteen years after the ANZAC landings, Mustafa Kemal Ataturk, Founder and first President of the modern Republic of Turkey, who had been Commander in Chief of the Turkish forces in Gallipoli, graciously responded to an Australian journalist's request and wrote, 'The landing at Gallipoli on 25 April 1915, and the fighting which took place on the peninsula will never be forgotten. They showed to the world the heroism of all those who shed their blood there. How heartrending for their nations were the losses that this struggle caused.' A century on, we, the people of both sides of that deadly struggle can gather, people of all faiths and none; we gather in peace, espousing the virtues of all who fought and daring to pray together for peace and reconciliation between us and amongst all peoples. We gather together helping each other to repair the heartrending and to prosper as best we can from the tragic, irreparable losses.

We remember the 130,000 who were killed on that blood-soaked peninsula during the Gallipoli campaign, and the other quarter of a million who were wounded. A century on, we have gathered more inclusively and not just to pray for the 44,000 Allies who died, but also for the 86,000 Turks who perished in their trenches opposite them. Being ANZAC Day, we particularly call to mind the 8709 Australians and 2779 Kiwis who died. A handful at the time were honoured by name for particular military feats, *'but of others there is no memory; they have perished as though they had never existed; but these also were godly men, whose righteous deeds have not been forgotten; their descendants stand by the covenants; and their glory will never be blotted out'*. (Ecclesiasticus 44:8-14)

We recall the innocence of the soldiers—many aged the same as many of those who today study here at Harvard—and the human values that they embodied of courage and mateship. We recall too the reality, routine and relentlessness of their fighting, their sufferings, and their deaths. We also recall the idealism, the hope, and perhaps even the naivety of empire which motivated and sustained them and those who sent them to battle. The ANZACs had sailed from Albany in Western Australia on All Saints Day, 1 November 1914. They waited in Egypt and then joined the Mediterranean Expeditionary Force of 75,000. They landed early morning, and in the wrong place. Because of navigational errors the ANZACs landed about 2 km north of the intended site. Instead of a flat stretch of coastline, the boats carrying the 1500 men who would make the first landing came ashore at what is now named appropriately Anzac Cove, a narrow beach overlooked by steep hills and ridgelines. Thus began an eight month campaign of combat in muddied trenches infested by lice, swarmed by flies, and putrified by faeces.

Back home, their political masters were sustained both by the pride of selfless colonial service to empire and by the hope of imminent military success. At 3pm on 29 April 1915, Australian Prime Minister Andrew Fisher rose in the House of Representatives and proudly declared:

> Some days ago the Australian War Expeditionary Forces were transferred from Egypt to the Dardanelles. They have since landed, and have been in action on the Gallipoli Peninsula. News reaches us that the action is proceeding satisfactorily. I am pleased to be able to read the following cablegram received to-day from the Secretary of State for the Colonies: —
>
> 'His Majesty's Government desire me to offer you their warmest congratulations on the splendid gallantry and magnificent achievement of your contingent in the successful progress of the operations at the Dardanelles.'
>
> To this the following reply has been despatched through His Excellency the Governor-General: —
>
> 'The Government and people of Australia are deeply gratified to learn that their troops have won distinction in their first encounter with the enemy. We are confident that they will carry the King's colours to further victory.'[1]

Next day Fisher read to the House a telegram from King George dated 29 April 1915:

> I heartily congratulate you upon the splendid conduct and bravery displayed by the Australian troops in the operations at the Dardanelles, who have indeed proved themselves worthy sons of the Empire.[2]

On 5 May 1915, ten days after the Gallipoli landing, Australian members of parliament were agitated that the Melbourne press were carrying details of New Zealand casualties but there were still no public details available of Australian casualties. A question was put to the Assistant Minister for Defence:

> In view of the many messages of congratulation that we have received regarding the bravery of our troops in action in the Dardanelle, is the Assistant Minister of Defence in a position

---

1. *Commonwealth Parliamentary Debates*, House of Representatives, 29 April 1915, 2724.
2. *Commonwealth Parliamentary Debates*, House of Representatives, 30 April 1915, 2814.

to tell the House with what result the bravery of our men has been attended?

The answer was simple, a huanting three words: *I am not.*[3]

Gradually, the political masters and then the people became apprised of the more gruesome reality on the other side of the globe. A century on, we balance the idealism of service to empire, the reality of death in the trenches, and the prospect of reconciliation with former enemies in scales which only grace and forgiveness can hold.

'Their bodies are buried in peace, but their names live on generation after generation. The assembly declares their wisdom, and the congregation proclaims their praise'. Despite the instability and the intractable conflicts on Turkey's borders today, we dare to gather in prayer dreaming of *'a new heaven and a new earth'* in which the God of Abraham, the God of Isaac, the God of Jacob *'will wipe every tear from their eyes'* so that *'mourning and crying and pain will be no more'*. (Revelation 21:4) We hear the word of Revelation proclaimed to all people of good will, to all peacemakers including those who have fought, those who are fighting, and those who will fight so that there might be no more war: *'I will be their God and they will be my children'*. (Revelation 21:7)

> Today, lest we forget.
> *They shall grow not old, as we that are left grow old:*
> *Age shall not weary them, nor the years condemn.*
> *At the going down of the sun and in the morning*
> *We will remember them.*

May the Aussies, the Kiwis and the Turks amongst us this morning go forth into Harvard Yard carrying and sharing the memories of those who encountered each other for the first time across trenches a century ago, committing ourselves afresh to transforming our heartrending and our losses into heartmending and tangible dividends of peace for our world.

Let's all pray in silence, each in their own way.

I will offer a Christian prayer:

---

3. *Commonwealth Parliamentary Debates*, House of Representatives, 5 May 1915, 2832.

Lord Our God, on this day, 100 years ago, the Australian and New Zealand Army Corps, at Gallipoli, made immortal the name of Anzac and established an imperishable tradition of selfless service, of devotion to duty, and of fighting for all that is best in human relationships.

O Lord, we who are gathered here today from both sides of that conflict remember with gratitude the men and women who have given, and are still giving all that is theirs to give, in order that the world may be a nobler place in which to live.

And with them, Lord, we remember those left behind to bear the sorrow of their loss.

We dedicate ourselves to taking up the burdens of the fallen and, with the same high courage and steadfastness with which they went into battle, to setting our hands to the tasks they left unfinished. Lord, we dedicate ourselves to the service of the ideals for which they died. With your help, O God, might we give our utmost to make the world what they would have wished it to be, a better and happier place for all of its people, through whatever means are open to us.

We make this prayer through Christ Our Lord. Amen.

8

The Enigma of Malcolm Fraser
(*Deceased 20 March 2015*)

Malcolm Fraser was always an enigma to me. But that's probably because I did not get to know him up close, all that well. With the departure of him and Gough Whitlam from the national stage in just five months, we are bereft of the leadership of elders who have known the highest elected office and who have lived long enough to share their wisdom immune from the partisanship of the day. Through the rough and tumble of politics, Fraser helped the country find true north on issues relating to race and human rights. He had the courage to question fundamental national preconceptions like the US alliance and border protection which placed the claims of boat people out of sight and out of mind.

Fraser started his political life as an establishment toff in the Liberal Party from the Western District of Victoria via Oxford. He enjoyed the ministerial leather at a very young age. At age thirty-six, he served as a minister first under Harold Holt, then under John Gorton until they fell out. And then William McMahon restored him to the Cabinet. I well remember reading Peter Howson's diaries which recount Howson's many ministerial lunches at the Melbourne Club. On 19 October 1971, Howson dined at the club with Fraser, recording: 'I warned him that Coombs had been talking with the PM, and that we might have to revise our views on traditional land rights. Malcolm indicated very firmly that he would not change his mind or the views he expressed in Cabinet last week.' Fraser was not for turning. Meanwhile Whitlam was pledging the Labor Party to national land rights. Within five years, Malcolm Fraser would be the prime minister trumpeting the passage of land rights legislation in the Northern Territory.

It is a tragedy that his prime ministership was permanently and irrevocably marred with the lack of legitimacy occasioned by the way he got there. Sir John Kerr did him no favour. No matter how many elections Fraser won, he could never cast off the tarnish which came from his complicity in a vice-regal initiative which required, if only for a moment, that the Leader of the Opposition be more privy to the mind of the Queen's representative than the Prime Minister commissioned to advise him. No matter how many High Court judges gave it the nod, this just would not wash with the general public as a credible sustainable constitutional arrangement. We are yet to put it right.

I well remember Barrie Dexter, the Secretary of the Department of Aboriginal Affairs, telling me: 'Of all the difficult regimes for which I had worked in Aboriginal Affairs, the Fraser Government was probably the harshest.' Dexter once wrote: 'Mr Fraser was an enigma. He sought some positive achievements in the field of Aboriginal affairs, but at the same time conducted an inquisition into, and almost destroyed, the Department—through which his desired achievements would have to be implemented!'

It is an eternal tribute to Malcolm Fraser that he stood by the key recommendations of the Woodward Royal Commission, taking on the recalcitrant Country Party, and insisting that the Parliament enact the Northern Territory Aboriginal land rights legislation. Fraser took many principled stands for human rights and against racial discrimination. He made substantive changes like setting up the Human Rights Commission. He made bold and principled appointments including my father and Sir William Deane to the High Court. Key authors of the *Mabo* judgment, they were later appointed chief justice and governor general respectively by Paul Keating.

I well recall the ceremony at the University of Technology Sydney 10 years after the *Mabo* decision when the Chancellor Sir Gerard Brennan, bestowing honorary doctorates on Malcolm Fraser and Sir William Deane, said: 'Today our nation stands in need of the kind of inspiration which our graduates of today have offered—a certain grandeur in public life, compassion for the marginalised in our own society and for those from other nations whom war or famine or persecution or poverty have robbed of human dignity, respect for the rule of law, commitment to an Australia that has pride in its place in the world.'

In the lead up to the 2007 election when emotions were running high about the Bali bombers, Robert McClelland, the Labor Shadow Attorney General, was copping Tory flak as well as Labor friendly fire for having made a principled statement against the death penalty. Fraser came out demonstrating how short sighted were his political successors saying, 'It is sad to see principle being thrown overboard and an expedient argument, which politicians believe will be the popular argument, pursued. So often matters of principle need to be explained and supported by those in positions of authority—and then, more often than not, those principles will find general support'.

In October 2009 he lent his considerable physical presence to the launch of our National Human Rights Consultation report recommending a national Human Rights Act for Australia as well as other procedures for better protecting human rights in Australia. It was well beyond the call of duty or personal allegiance for him to be there. His sheer presence provided inspiration and hope for the many young people who thought Australia needed to do better in protecting and enhancing human rights.

His friendship with Gough Whitlam has been one of the great signs in Australian public life that human decency and shared commitment to noble ideals can transcend even the most entrenched political animosities cultivated across the despatch box, even when those animosities are exacerbated by vice regal intrigue with judicial warrant. Now that all the principal actors in the 1975 dismissal are deceased might we now put right our defective constitutional arrangements which caused irremediable harm to Kerr, Whitlam and Fraser. We owe it to ourselves but also to them so that their finest achievements might outshine the darkness of that fracture in the nation's constitutional architecture.

9

The Quirkiness of Wayne Goss
(*Deceased 10 November 2014*)

Those of us brought up in Queensland owe a lot to Wayne Goss. I first met him when he was instrumental in setting up the Aboriginal Legal Service (ALS) in Brisbane in 1974. He was the articled clerk. Roisin Hirschfeld was a young social worker at the ALS. They later married and their two children went on to become Rhodes scholars. With Mark Plunkett, I used go in one day a week to the ALS as a volunteer law student. Matt Foley was there in the wings too. (Plunkett went on to sue Joh Bjelke-Petersen for conspiracy to pervert the course of justice when the police commissioner was precluded from investigating assaults on student demonstrators. Foley became Attorney General in the Goss government.)

Wayne was a no nonsense fellow with a real commitment to justice for Aboriginal Australians during the difficult Bjelke-Petersen days in Queensland. He had a quirkish and devilish sense of humour. He put himself on the line, committed to legal representation for indigent Aborigines, appearing constantly in the courts, day in and day out. He would always come back to the office with a smile and a joke about the latest put down he suffered at the hands of the unforgiving magistrate not much given to pleas invoking past dispossession. He was irrepressible. He delighted in the quirks of human nature, especially from the bench, and later in the parliamentary chamber. He knew there had to be a better way.

In 1989, seeing off Joh Bjelke-Petersen who had been rolled by his own, he beat the National Party at the polls and was elected premier. In his first term, he decided to do something about Aboriginal land rights in the most difficult state of the federation. He did this when there was no political or legal imperative to do so. He acted because he believed it was right. He believed in Aboriginal self-determination within the life of the polity. He retained the services of two young Aborigines to advise him—Noel Pearson and Marcia Langton. His chief bureaucratic adviser was Kevin Rudd.

As ever, he proceeded cautiously attempting to balance all interests. He announced his 'modest, blanched and responsible' land-rights package telling the Queensland public: 'We rejected out of hand the Northern Territory approach as being too radical both in the way it affects the community generally and the specific impact on agriculture and mining.'

Despite his best efforts, things turned sour and Aborigines knocked down the gates of the Queensland Parliament House. He was understandably very hurt, but philosophical about the course of post-colonial relations. Wayne was unerring in his commitment to do what he could to alleviate the unjust plight of the first Australians. He was no starry eyed romantic. He never lost his sense of humour, or his unwavering commitment to justice for the first Australians.

In 2011, I appeared with Wayne on the negative side of one of those 'Intelligence Squared' debates. By this time Wayne had gone under the knife repeatedly, taking on the brain tumour that finally took him. He was as quirky and good humoured as ever. The topic was: 'If we populate, we perish'. The chief protagonist for the 'yes' case was Dick Smith who turned up with lots of free copies of his book *Population Crisis* which he distributed to the audience. Wayne responded:

> Ladies and Gentlemen, because you are a sophisticated audience, our team has decided that we will not be offering bribes in the form of free books nor will we be trying to scare the pants off you with predictions of the end of the planet. We believe that the policy debate should be lifted to a higher level. What I think I need to do is to reframe the issue: if Australia does not increase its population, you know what will happen? We'll get older; we'll get less productive; we'll lose our spark. You know what happens after you age and get greyer and greyer and greyer? You perish. Think about it.

His last words in that debate were, 'Friends, Australia has a great opportunity. Let's seize it.' He did and so should we. I was honoured to know him. He was a very honourable man.

10.

The Grandeur of Gough Whitlam
(*Deceased 21 October 2014*)

Gough Whitlam once asked me why there were so many social reformers to emerge from Queensland in the early 1970s. I told him it was simple. We had someone to whom we could react: Sir Joh Bjelke Petersen; and we had someone to inspire us: him. I have written elsewhere about his contribution to Aboriginal rights, human rights and international law. Here, I reflect on the man who inspired me so affectionately, so supportively, and with such a sense of fun. What he did for me, he did for countless other Australians who dreamt of a better world and a nobler Australia. Even his political opponents are forever in his debt for having elevated the national vision and for having given us a more complete and generous image of ourselves. A few days after his death, I happened to visit the Museum of Fine Arts in Boston. I took the afternoon tour of American art. With pride, our guide ended the tour with Jackson Pollock's painting *No 10*. I was able to tell her it was not a patch on *Blue Poles* purchased by a visionary prime minister down under who copped all hell for spending a six figure sum on just one painting. That was our Gough. We are forever in his debt.

I will share three vignettes.

In 1980, I took a busload of boys from Xavier College to Canberra on a politics tour. Andrew Peacock was their local member. They gave him a hard time because of Malcolm Fraser's boycott of the Olympics. I was anxious for them to meet Whitlam who was by then a visiting scholar at the Australian National University writing his large tome on the Whitlam years. The boys, many of whom came from households very sympathetic to the politics of B A Santamaria, were testy. Why did I want them to travel across town to meet a 'has been'? They had met their fill of politicians up at Parliament

House. Gough wowed them. First he gave them morning tea; then he fielded their questions. The burly Dan Hess, with a passing wink to his school mates, asked, 'What was it like to be sacked?' Gough drew back and then moved forward, telling the young Christian gentlemen that the events of 1975 had to be seen in the context of the decline in traditions and institutions in our society. He then asked a rhetorical question in conclusion, 'For example, how many of you boys from Xavier College would ever contemplate becoming a Jesuit nowadays?' No one answered, but the remark had some impact on the now Fr Edward Dooley SJ.

In 1981, Gough was awarded an honourary doctorate of letters. I had written congratulating him on his receipt of an honour which was both appropriate and ideologically sound. I did not hear back from him for some months, and I had no expectation of any response. Then some months later again, he worked his way across a crowded room to speak to me. We both had the advantage of being considerably taller than most of our companions in a crowd. He asked, 'Did you get my letter?' I told him how pleased and honoured I was. He asked, 'Did it arrive with Vatican stamps?' Indeed it had. He had instructed the embassy officials in Rome that the letter had to be posted from the Vatican. The envelope bore the crest of the English College. The letter commenced with words to this effect: 'It is with great pleasure that I write you this, my first letter from the Romans, and I do so from the most fashionable address in the eternal city.'

In late 1997, I landed at Sydney airport, having flown in from Broome, and was about to make my way back to St Canice's Church in Kings Cross. Gough and the good 'Dame Margaret' (as he liked to refer to his beloved) were there. He offered me a lift in their government limousine. On arrival at the church, I asked whether he liked mangoes as I had some splendid ones from the Kimberley. He replied, 'I do, and Dame Margaret loves them.' A few weeks later, I was preparing for the funeral of Nugget Coombs in St Marys Cathedral Sydney. There had been a little tension in the background between Prime Minister John Howard's office and Aboriginal leader Patrick Dodson about what should be said in Dodson's eulogy about Aboriginal self-determination and conflict with government. It was at the height of controversy over the *Wik* ten point plan. Some last minute changes were made to Dodson's text. With only minutes to spare, I made it out onto the front steps of the cathedral to welcome the official mourning party including Mr Howard, Mr Dodson and Sir William Deane. The TV cameras were in close proximity. Then up the steps came Gough oblivious of all controversy. He grasped me firmly by the hand and with that glint in the eye said, 'Father, the mangoes were magnificent.' It was a blessed moment.

During the service, Gough, who was fond of describing himself as 'a fellow traveller—not so much a pillar of the Church but rather one of those flying buttresses you find on European cathedrals', came up onto the sanctuary to deliver his own eulogy. This is how he commenced: 'Prime Ministers like to describe themselves as the servants of the people. The most striking claim of the Supreme Pontiff is to be the servant of the servants of God. If, in this setting and as the last of the seven Prime Ministers whom Coombs served, I were to suggest an epitaph for him, it would be "the servant of the servants of the people".' Everyone laughed; we were all at ease; Gough was in command. He concluded that eulogy with words I now apply to him:

> At some time or in some place or in some way the life of everybody in this gathering and in our country would have been touched by Nugget's manifold activities and enriched by his talents. He was given many talents. He produced great dividends on them. All Australians can say, in the words of the parable, 'Well done, thou good and faithful servant'.

We can all join a chorus of 'Amen, Alleluia' to that. Farewell loyal friend of many, dedicated leader of the nation, and visionary servant of the people in the great south land of the Holy Spirit.

Conclusion

Soon after my return to Australia following upon a year's sojourn in wintry Boston, I attended the annual reception at the Apostolic Nunciature in Canberra. This is an event attended by diplomats and community leaders. The formalities consist of the papal nuncio, who is the personal representative of the Pope, proposing a toast to the Queen and people of Australia. In response, the most senior civil leader present proposes a toast to the Pope. For the first time in memory, no federal ministers were in attendance. They had certainly been invited. They all had other priorities. The reciprocal toast was proposed by a public servant. I understand there were no federal ministers in attendance when the new Catholic Archbishop was installed in St Mary's Cathedral, Sydney a few months before. And this, despite there being a large number of Catholics in the Abbott ministry. There's a lot of change going on in Australia. People do not join institutions like churches or clubs as they did in the past. The churches are losing their moral authority in the community. Politicians do not feel the same need to be attentive to church voices. People in the pews no longer feel obliged to follow the clerical instructions from the pulpit. It is time for those of us in the Church to stop paying undue deference to those who exercise ecclesiastical power in a fashion at odds with contemporary notions of transparency and equality.

In his book *After Virtue*, the American political philosopher Alasdair MacIntyre despairs about many of the developments in North America and Europe. No doubt he would detect many of the same developments in Australia. He cautions against drawing parallels with the decline of the Roman Empire but he does note some. He writes, 'A crucial turning point in that earlier history occurred when men and women of goodwill turned aside from the task of shoring up the Roman *imperium* and ceased to identify the continuation of civility and moral community with the maintenance of the *imperium*. What they set themselves to achieve instead was the construction of new forms of community within which the moral life could be sustained so that both morality and civility might survive the coming barbarism and darkness.' MacIntyre is not an outright pessimist. He is confident that the tradition of the virtues can sustain us in season and out of season. He does warn rather melodramatically, 'This time however the barbarians are not waiting beyond the frontiers; they have already been governing us for quite some time.' His concern is not any particular political party or ideology. He urges, 'What matters at this stage is the construction of local forms of community within which civility and the intellectual and moral life can be sustained through the new dark ages which are already upon us.'[1]

MacIntyre's critique of liberalism is derived from 'a judgment that the best type of human life, that in which the tradition of the virtues is most adequately embodied, is lived by those engaged in constructing and sustaining forms of community directed towards the shared achievement of those common goods without which the ultimate human good cannot be achieved.'[2]

If we are to make prudent judgments and take appropriate action in relation to issues such as climate change, security, migration, and economic growth in a globalised world, we need leaders who can appeal to the public's finer nature, idealistic selves, and longer term vision. Short term electoral gain by appealing to individualistic self-interest or collective fear of the 'other' just won't cut it. These leaders need to be plugged into the new and emerging communities of discourse which can inform and sustain morality and civility regardless of the waning influence of churches and more traditional groupings which have helped to form leaders in the past. Our new leaders will be emerging from new networks of virtue and will be wrestling with novel moral questions which require attentiveness to the wishes and demands of the electorate as well as to the aspirations and entitlements of those who are disenfranchised either because

---

1. Alisdair MacIntyre, *After Virtue: A Study in Moral Theory*, University of Notre Dame Press, 3rd edition, 2007, p 263.
2. Ibid, p xiv.

they are outside national borders or they are vulnerable at the edges of life and community.

Gough Whitlam in his book *The Whitlam Government 1972-1975* quotes Machiavelli's *The Prince*: 'And one has to reflect that there is nothing more difficult to handle nor more doubtful of success nor more dangerous to conduct than to make oneself the leader in introducing a new order of things.' Whitlam of course pledged his faith to his own political party which provided him with the contours of a popular, coherent political ideology. Those contours are falling away in all major political parties, and the lines of demarcation between the major parties are now movable and blurred. Whitlam was on firmer permanent ground when he said, 'It is now a question of maintaining the faith, the faith in the possibility of achievable and enduring reforms towards the great goals of a more equal, more independent, more tolerant Australia' as well as 'faith in parliamentary democracy as the means of achieving those reforms'.[3] Our elected political leaders will be assisted in the task of national change by the input of those other conscientious community leaders who are freer to espouse ideals or perspectives which are focused on the common good of the planet and of all humanity, even though these concerns do not presently win majority support at the ballot box. Our church leaders will assist in so far as they are able to engage with the vast array of community members not in their pews and unfamiliar with their theological preconceptions. And women will need to be appropriately represented at the table, whether in Cabinet or at a papal consistory.

---

3. Gough Whitlam, *The Whitlam Government 1972-1975*, Penguin Books, 1985, p 744.

Index

A
Aboriginal deaths in custody, 34.
Aboriginal land rights, 72, 75.
Andrews, Kevin, 5.
ANZAC Day, 65, 66, 68.
Asylum policy, 53, 58.
Ataturk, Mustafa Kemal, 65.
Australian Christian Lobby, 48.

B
Badham, Van, xi.
Barwick, Garfield, 47, 48.
Benedict XVI, Pope, 20, 21.
Bjelke-Petersen, Joh, 75.
Bongiorno, Paul, ix–xii.
Brennan, Gerard, 72.
Burke, Tony, 57.

C
Callinan, Ian, 20.
Chifley, Joseph Benedict, xi, xii, xvi, 41–63.
Child Sexual Abuse, xvi, xvii, 17–28.
Clark, Vicki, 36.
Cohen, Leonard, 63.
Communist Party Dissolution Case, 59.
Conaci, Francis Xavier, 36.
Coombs, HC, 71, 78, 79.
Corrs Chambers Westgarth, Solicitors, 17, 25.
Cremin, David, 33.
Cunneen, Margaret, 18.
Curtin, John, 43, 51, 53.

D
Dada, Carlos, 32.
Dalzell, John, 24.
David McIver, 43.44.
Deane, William, vii, 72, 79.
Debt Conversion Agreement Bill 1931, 50.
Dexter, Barrie, 72.
Dirimera, John Baptist, 36.
Dodson, Patrick, 78, 79.
Donovan, Thomas, 5.
Dooley, Edward, 78.
Downer, Alexander, 56.
Duggan, Aidan, 17, 18, 23.

E

El Salvador, 29, 30, 31, 32.
Ellacuria, Ignacio, 31.
Ellis Case, 17, 18, 22–27.
Evans, Chris, 58.
Evatt, HV, 43, 59.

F

Faircloth, Sean, 8.
Federation of Asian Bishops Conference, 7.
Fiduciary Bill 1931, 50.
Fisher, Andrew, 66, 67.
Fisher, Anthony, 26, 27.
Foley, Matthew, 75.
Forché, Carolyn, 29, 31.
Francis, Pope, xii, xiii, xvi, xvii, 6, 8, 9, 10, 15, 16, 30, 31, 32, 36.
Fraser, Malcolm, xi, xv, xvii, 44, 71, 72, 73, 77.

G

Gallipoli, 65, 66, 67, 68.
George V, King, 67.
Geraghty,Chris, 35.
Gillard, Julia, xii, xvi, 41, 42, 43, 55, 57.
Gleeson, Gerald, 17, 25.
Globalisation, 6.
Goss, Wayne, 75, 76.
Grande, Rutillio, 29, 31.
Grayling, AC, 8.
Griffin, Walter Burley, 5, 12.

H

Harradine, Brian, 45, 46.
Harvard Memorial Church, 65.
Heiss, Elsie, 36.
Hess, Dan, 78.
Heythrop College, 11.
Hirschfeld, Roisin, 75.
Holt, Harold, 71.
Houston Panel, 56, 57.
Howard, John, xii, 45, 57, 78, 79.
Howson, Peter, 71.
Humanae Vitae, 10.

I

Ignatius Loyola, 13, 14, 15, 16.

J

Johnson, Elizabeth, 11.

K

Keating, Paul, xii, xiii, 45, 46, 72.
Kennedy, John F, xi,
Kennedy, Ted, 33.
Kerr, John, 72, 73.
King, Martin Luther, 34.

L

L'Estrange, Peter, 5, 13.
Lang, Jack, 43, 50, 51, 53.
Langton, Marcia, 76.
Laudato Si', 6, 10, 16.
Light on the Hill, xii, xvi, 41–63.

Locatelli, Paul, 6, 7.
Luchetti, Tony, 53, 59.

M

Mabo decision, 45, 72.
MacIntyre, Alisdair, 81, 82.
MacKillop, Mary, 36.
Malaysia Solution, 53, 55, 56, 57.
Mannix, Daniel, 3, 4, 5, 12.
Marriage Act 1961, 46, 47, 48.
McClelland, Robert, 73.
McMahon, William, 71.
Menzies, Robert Gordon, 59.
Monan, Donald, 31.
Morris, William, xii, 19, 20, 21, 22, 27, 28.
Morrison, Scott, 57.
Mundine, Graham, 36.

N

National Human Rights Consultation, 73.
Native Title, 45.
Nauiyu Nambiyu, 33.
Nauru, 54, 56, 57.
Newman College, 3, 4, 5, 11.
Niall, Brenda, 3, 4, 5.
Nicolas, Adolfo, 6, 7.

O

O'Donoghue, Lowitja, 45.
O'Dwyer, James, 4.
O'Malley, John, 10, 11.

P

Paul VI, Pope, 10.
Peacock, Andrew, 77.
Pearson, Noel, xv, 45, 76.
Pell, George, 17, 19, 21, 22, 23, 24, 26, 28.
Phan, Peter, 7.
Plunkett, Mark, 75.
Pollock, Jackson, 77.

R

Rayner, Brian, 22, 23.
Redfern, 33, 34.
Refugee Convention, 54, 55, 58.
Robinson, Geoffrey, xiii.
Romero, Oscar, 29, 30, 31, 32, 34.
Roosevelt, Theodore, xv.
Royal Commission into Institutional Responses to Child Sexual Abuse, 17–27.
Rudd, Kevin, xii, xiii, xvi, 41, 42, 43, 45, 46, 55, 56, 57, 76.

S

Salvado, Rosendo, 36.
Same sex marriage, 46, 48, 49.
Santamaria, Bob, 46, 77.
Scullin, Joseph, 50, 53.
Shorten, Bill, 48, 60.
Smith, Dick, 76.
St Paul's Outside the Walls, 36.
Stopping the boats, xvi, 53, 56, 57, 58.

T

Towards Healing, 17, 19, 24, 25, 26, 27.
Truth Justice and Healing Council, 26.

U

UN Declaration of Human Rights, 54.
Ungunmerr, Miriam Rose, 33.
Untener, Ken, 32.

W

Whitlam, Gough, xi, xii, xv, xvii, 47, 71, 73, 83.
Whitlam, Margaret, 78.
Wik decision, 45, 78.
Woodward Royal Commission, 72.
Wright, George, 41, 42, 62.
Wynn-Pope, Phoebe, xv.

Lightning Source UK Ltd.
Milton Keynes UK
UKOW01f0442070218
317473UK00002B/205/P